A GUIDE TO THE HELDERBERG & HOTTENTOTS HOLLAND MOUNTAIN RIM

Mountains, Trails, History, Legends, Caves, Rock Art and Rock Climbs

BY STEVE CHADWICK

2nd Edition • March 2023 Revised and extended • © Steve Chadwick
Design & Layout: Richard smith

Sunset beyond the Strand and False Bay from high up the mountainside

Preface

The Heidelberg Basin enjoys a backcloth of magnificence – the Helderberg / Hottentots Holland Mountain Rim. Our own self-important lives are but flashes of milliseconds compared to the ages these monoliths have stood and endured. High above us lie serrated rows of peaks that are cut by dramatic kloofs, the tops of which are often hidden in a white blanket as the frenetic south-easter pumps thick white clouds over the mountains and through the neks.

When winter comes, water courses that dried out in summer fill with heavy rains and disgorge in torrents down the mountainside. Damp patches become sodden high mountain catchments. Rivulets appear in the soaked rocky soil and gather into streams that become surging cascades tumbling down kloofs. We see dramatic 'grey mares' tails' as the wind drives these streams back up the mountain faces as spray.

There are not that many places in the world where you can live surrounded by mountains – to watch the rising sun peep over the peaks or crawl slyly up through a nek. Or in the evening to enjoy the light show as the setting sun caresses the mountain face with crimson blushes.

Sometimes, on warm summer nights, friends and I trek up to higher places to watch the sunset. Then we chill awhile and play some cool acoustic music while the rising full moon's silvery light casts its cold shadows. It's almost as bright as day as the moon rises over those same mountains that the sunset blushes have just left - double whammy of eye-candy fantasia.

In summer's heat the mountains shimmer above us, seeming to taunt us: 'Come on up, it's nice here!' Hikes in the summer are chosen with care, as the mountain traveller needs to be careful of that very same heat. There may be no respite from the sun, no shade, and maybe no water for kilometres. Humidity on a morning climb up a steep slope, combined with unrelenting heat can be a recipe for heat exhaustion or worse. Like any wild place on the surface of the earth, our mountains are beautiful, but must be treated with respect. Nature may punish anyone for disrespect and lack of foresight.

Driven by curiosity, I have spent many years slowly gathering data regarding the Helderberg / Hottentots Holland Rim. I am guilty of becoming increasingly passionate in my search, and have lately been encouraged by friends to collect all my research in one place, in case the history and stories are lost forever.

Along the way I have had help and encouragement from many people. I would like to thank members of the Gantouw Hike Club and the Mountain Club of South Africa Hottentots Holland section. Thanks, as well to Muriel Rowcroft, Denise Fourie and

Playing some mellow songs whilst the full moon rises.

Full moon rise soon after sunset between Langkloofberg and Moordenaarskop.

Rossouw Nel for patient proof reading. Leslie Downie, Frans Slabber, Stu Summerfield, Mike O'Keefe, Ron du Toit and David Wright for their encouragement and support. I also thank younger members of the MCSA who have taken on the task of checking routes in remote places that I didn't manage to get to before my own joints, worn by many decades of mountain climbing and hiking, would no longer allow me to access, namely Dante Visser, Rossouw Nel, Nico van Der Watt, Raphael Shaw and Evan Kortje.

Much of the land noted in this guide is under private ownership or in Nature reserve management. As such much route data is written for posterity. Individual groups would need to obtain access permission.

I have been collecting pictures for this publication for some eight years. Most unsubscribed pictures are my own, but over the years I have lost track of the originators of some of the pictures. I apologise if any of the photos are not correctly credited. Please mail me and I will correct in any future editions.

Any perceived corrections and/or additional information will be gratefully received. Send to: slioch980@gmail.com.

It is my earnest hope that readers will have as much fun as I have had and be as fascinated as I have been in teasing out the intriguing stories and history of the mountains that tower above us.

Note: Walks and climbs in this guide demand a certain degree of care from those using it. The author will in no way be held liable for any damage or injury that might occur using this guide.

Let the journey round the Rim begin!
Steve Chadwick • November 2022

Grading used in this book

Contentious though this may be, it was long thought by some that the two-digit grading system did not fully inform hikers of the what they would getting into. Such that two local clubs collaborated to produce a grading system that lets the hiker know three important but often very separate items.

We adopted the MCSA standard for effort - how much energy one would expect to expend. An alpha system of A, B, C and D was adopted for Exposure (fear factor).
Traffic lights were adopted for denoting Technical difficulty.

Exertion	Exposure to height	Technical difficulty
1. Relatively easy	**A.** None	🟩 Easy hiking, walking on a trail with occasional use of hands (if applicable)
2. Moderate	**B.** Some	🟧 Easy scrambling, walking on or off path with frequent use of hands required
3. Strenuous	**C.** Exposed	🟥 Scrambling – frequent use of hands to facilitate upward movement
4. For the very fit	**D.** Very exposed	⬛ Serious scrambling A rope may be necessary

Content

Kingdom of the Gods	1
Helderbergplass and West Peak	3
Helderberg Nature Reserve	7
Helderberg Nature Reserve West Peak and the Dome	11
Suurberg	23
Haelkop	24
Pic-Sans-Nom & the Triplets	28
Somerset Sneeukop	32
Sneeukop's Maclear's Beacon	37
Sneeukop outriders. Pisgah, Sneekopnaald, Landdrosnaald	43
Valleiberg, Langklippiek, Langkloofberg	45
Diepgat to Sneeukopkloof	48
Katjieboskloof to the N2	57
History of Sir Lowry's Pass	71
A shard of pottery	81
History of the Ox wagons	84
N2 to the sea	90

Addendums: 99

Rock art, Cape point to the HH Rim	99
Running the rim guide	107
Rock climbing guide Hottentots Holland Rim	119
Hottentots Holland Anomaly	140
Basic Guide to Evac / Rescue Procedure	144
Snake bite first aid	146
Heat Exhaustion	150

Kingdom of the Gods

Most of us would admit to having had a spiritual connection with the mountains at some time or other. We look up at the mountains and are moved by their rugged majestic beauty because we have made a connection with nature. Some would say that we have connected with the spirit of the mountain itself.

It may be a view you have seen many times, but weather, light and time of day makes it different every time. The rising sun and its movement changes our view throughout the day. During the mountain's darker moods, cloud swirls around the tops, cascading down the flanks to dissipate as the tendrils feather out and disappear.

When I was in Cape Town a few days ago, old Van Hunks must have been puffing his pipe very well, as the 'tablecloth' was in good form whirling and pouring down the mountain flank. We often see the same thing here in Somerset West when the raging south-easter pushes banks of clouds over the Hottentots, and the cloud tumbles down the kloofs and neks.

Then there are the sunsets, with the mountains' flanks set aglow in shades of crimson as the setting sun plunges into the sea off Cape Town, but not before giving us a last display to take our breath away.

There are those 'mystics' or believers in theosophy, often followers of Buddhist or Brahmanic beliefs, that say they can see spirits in the mountains – the kingdom of the angelic hosts, known in the East as the kingdom of the Devas, or 'the Shining Ones'.

Such a man was Geoffrey Hodson, born 12 March 1886 and died 23 January 1983. He is believed by some to be one of the greatest occultists of the period.

Geoffrey Hodson wrote several books regarding his beliefs, and while visiting South Africa in 1937 to stay with friends, Mr and Mrs Quail and their daughter Ethelwynne, he saw a spirit above the Hottentots Holland Mountains. Hodson described what he saw to Ethelwynne, who then proceeded to draw the spirit or god that Geoffrey described.

In his book 'The Kingdom of the Gods' Hodson writes:

'This picture portrays the presiding God of the mountain range, which was observed high above one of the peaks of the Hottentots Holland Mountains…….as I observed

and gave my description to the artist, the downflow of power was so great and so brilliant as almost to conceal the form and aura of the God. The chief colours were lavender, gold and white, the central form of the God and the aura immediately surrounding it shining in those hues with a dazzling radiance quite impossible to reproduce.

The uprush of golden-coloured fiery power above the head was particularly brilliant, bestowing upon the God the appearance of a majestic Diva King wearing a crown of flames……however prodigious the outpouring of power may be, the God always gives the impression of complete mastery of the forces flowing through and about it. The central figure was at least eighty feet (24m) tall.'

The composition by Ethelwynne, as she drew what was described by Geoffrey Hodson.

I have held this topic on file until prompted by seeing this stunning picture by Murray Williams. The Diva or 'Shining One' seems to come out of the photograph. I am a realist, though also a romantic, so Murray's beautiful picture moved me to write this piece.

Photo courtesy of Murray Willams

References:
Hodson, Geoffrey. 1972. Kingdom of the Gods. Quest Books
Murray Williams
Theosophy World resource centre.

Helderberg Plaas and West Peak

There is a general rule that guidebook descriptions work from left to right when describing an area. This suits us fine as it means we may commence with an area that is close to the heart of many Helderberg basin residents and visitors, and begin our rim guide with the West Peak and the Dome. Those two majestic peaks that form part of a chain of seven Helderberg tops that rise high above the Helderberg Nature Reserve, before the ridge drops down into Grootnek at 540m.

Laying at the toe of the very left-hand side of the Helderberg / Hottentots Holland Mountain Rim we have:

A diadem of fire, taken during the evening of 11th June 2022. Pic courtesy of Roxanne Leipsig

Helderberg Plaas

The farm is known to many of us as a place to call in to purchase in season delicious strawberries, and to perhaps relax under the trees in the tea garden or braai site. Access is by a turn off from the R44 Somerset West to the Klein Helderberg road.

In 1692 the farm, originally called Moddergatsberge, was granted by Governor Simon van der Stel to Klaas Vechtman. In return, as was the norm, Klass had to deliver part of his wheat crop to the 'Compagnie'. In 1843 the farm passed to the Hendriksz / Obermeyer family; in whose charge it has remained for 6 generations.

Helderberg Plaas is open Mondays to Sundays 08:00 – 17:00. Closed on Good Friday & Christmas day. Current entry charge for hikers is R35. Children to 18 years, and pensioners benefit by a R25 charge. Annual permits are also available.

The object of this guide is to talk of the high places, so although the farm offers several walks of differing lengths, we are only concerned here with the most direct route up to West Peak.

An idyllic place that Helderbergplaas calls 'The Dam'.

The farm has gone to some lengths to keep vehicle 4x4, mountain bike and hike trails separate, and hikers are asked to respect this differentiation for their own safety and convenience. Hikers are also asked not to stray off hiking trails.

Once your hike fee has been paid, your vehicle may be left parked outside the farm shop, or you may drive around to park tidily at the excess parking area.

The hiking trail starts at the Tea Garden entrance, pick up the 'green' footprints leading to the dam. Now follow the 'red' footprints trail past the delightful dam, with its trees overhanging the water which is complete with water lilies.

Continue to follow the red feet until you reach the red and yellow feet interchange. Now follow the ever-steepening hill up to a loop bend left then back right, until you can see the wooden viewing platform up to your left. A great site for a sustenance break. Picnics on the view decking to be booked and paid for in advance

Go through the gate behind you and follow the 'blue' footprints looping jeep track until you reach the communication towers.

You may pass these gaunt steel pylons to climb the steep loose braided trail slope directly above you until you reach the rock face where the ascending trail from HNR joins you from your right; but this route is discouraged in favour of the recommended option – which will give the braded worn trail above a chance to regenerate.

Take the jeep track left from the towers for some 200m to pick up an easier angled zigzag ascent that climbs at an easier angle before crossing back right to the same junction with the trail that climbs up from HNR.

West Peak by any direction is a good grade 3B Orange. Which means 3 out of 4 for effort, B for some exposure, and Orange for some hands-on scrambling.

The route to West Peak now follows a series of slightly exposed but easy enough ledges and steps left round the flank of the mountain spur to gain the south west ridge of West Peak.

The route to the summit along this ridge may be taken direct by mild scrambling. Post June 2022 fire the HNR crew has done an excellent job in re-marking the trail up this south-west ridge of the mountain. The right-and south east (HNR) side is very precipitous and must be avoided.

Some of the older threads of trails on the lower west side can be extremely misleading especially on descent. It is advised to keep to the marked trail.

It should be noted that descending West Peak by its north east ridge (towards the Dome) is not recommended, as this would necessitate descending Porcupine Ridge, which is steep and contains several damp rocky sections. The Porcupine Ridge trail post fire was re-opened on Saturday 12th Nov 2022, after much hard work by HNR staff. Such that the ascent of West Peak (anti-clockwise) by this routre is again an option.

Looking towards the Dome from the summit of West Peak 1,003 m. As with any mountain, be spatially aware of where you are and the way down, as bad weather can set in.

Helderberg Nature Reserve

A brief history of the Helderberg Nature Reserve

The purpose of this guide is record everything 'high'. Having said that, the fact that Helderberg Nature Reserve plays such an important part in the life of many people in the Helderberg basin, I thought it may be of interest to readers and users of HNR if I note a little of the history that led to our being able to appreciate this gem on our doorstep.

The story of the reserve that we enjoy today begins with the demise of Simon van der Stel and his son Willem Adriaan.

Commander Simon van der Stel and his family arrived in Cape Town in October 1679. His son Willem held several important posts in the growing Cape Town administration before returning to Amsterdam. In 1699 Willem van der Stel returned to the Cape to take over as Governor from his retiring father.

Unfortunately, following the maxim that 'power corrupts', both father and son took part in several self-aggrandisement ventures. Among them being the compelling of bakers to buy wheat from the Stel family as a monopoly at inflated prices, the accepting of bribes for the granting of title-deeds, and the gaining of land by granting title-deeds to friends, then buying the land from those friends at very low prices. In such ways the family gradually acquired wealth as well as obtaining much of the productive land within the Hottentots Holland rim.

By 1705, the burghers had had enough of this misuse of power, and led by Adam Tas a list of grievances was drawn up that was signed by a great many of the free burghers of the area. This document was kept in safe keeping, for Willem van der Stel got wind of the document and tried to find and destroy it. The document reached Amsterdam and the VOC (Dutch East India Country) sent a copy to Willem with a request that he answer the charges.

Try to wriggle out of it - though the van der Stel family did - the order finally came in 1709 that the 'Stel' estate be sold in lots and that the area be returned to 'law and order'. An area comprising portions of the Lourensford and 'Erin Vale' (two words at this time) were bought by Jacobus van der Heiden.

By 1813, an area of '117 morgen' was bought by Hendrik Henriksz, and the area became known as 'Land-en-Zeezight' – 'land and sea view'.

By 1849 Land-en-Zeezight passed to Hendriks eldest son Johannes who died in 1883, after which the estate passed jointly to his sons Daniel and Johannes.

The oak trees that give us shade as we our park our cars in the reserve were planted by Daniel and Johannes as a wind break.

On the deaths of Daniel and Johannes, ownership passed to their niece Helena Louw.

In 1947 in order to create a reservoir and to generally improve the consistency of the growing towns water supply the municipality of Somerset West acquired the estate known as Land-en-Zeezicht from Mrs Helena Catharina Louw.
Once the land was under municipal ownership, several bodies felt that the land should also be used for the general good of the people of the Helderberg basin. In particular the Rotary Club was instrumental in proposing plans, and undertook to raise between R6,000 and R10,000 to support the proposal.

In the interim period, the Council set up an initial meeting of the 'Helderberg Nature Reserve' and an advisory body was set up on the 18th January 1960, at which councillors and representitives of various interested bodies met and agreed a framework.

Dr Douglas Hey - Director of Nature Conservation — was invited to advise the board, and on the 20th June 1960 Dr Hey applied to the Administrator of the Cape Province for formal provision of the reserve.

The request for the Reserve was accepted by the Administrator of the Cape Province such that proclamation no. 3268 was approved on the 23rd September 1960, and the 'Land-en-Zeezicht Nature Reserve' came into being. Though the local name soon became the 'Helderberg Nature Reserve'.

The Administrator of the Cape, His Honour Mr JN Malan officially opened the reserve on 3rd October 1964.

In 1974 the large earth reservoir was constructed near the southern boundary of the reserve, and the reservoir is still in operation — the City of Cape Town Bulk Water Branch manages this facility and water is extracted from the reservoir and treated on a daily basis to supply water to the Somerset West area and beyond.

Many of the old paths and tracks on the mountainside have been revealed due to the 11/12 Jun 2022 fire, indicating a long period of practical use, mostly for water conservation purposes.

Immediately post the 1964 opening of HNR the only paths that existed lay in the lower portion of the reserve, but gradually vehicle tracks were made up the hillside, sometimes making use of the older tracks.

The myriad of old tracks and irrigation ducts built in preceding years revealed clearly by the 11/12/Jun 2022 fire.

Linking trails of Caracal and the higher trails of Leopards and Woodies soon came into being. The vehicle track into Disa gorge, itself an offshoot of the upper right Protea track, was only opened in 1981.

In 1995 the reserve was enlarged by the addition of a 122-hectare portion above the Erinvale Country Golf Course. This was made possible by a 99-year lease from the Lourensford Estate. The Watsonia vehicle track on this ground soon followed. The linking trail of Baboons Traverse crossing from high on Watsonia to Disa was soon unofficially opened up by hikers, and was officially added to HNR's list of hikes in 2014.

The restaurant was built in 1964 and enlarged in 1994 to its present size. At the time of writing (April 2022) this watering hole is closed. We hope this much-loved resting spot will soon be reopened. In 1996 the original Environmental Education Centre was built.

The ground-breaking new Interpretive Centre has recently been erected and the building was officially opened on 3 June 2022.

The Friends of the Helderberg Nature Reserve (FHNR) came into being in 1986, and have been instrumental in supporting the HNR ever since.

Currently the upper section of the mountain, roughly delineated by the line of the Leopards trail, falls under the jurisdiction of the Cape Nature; though in reality the Staff of HNR with additional support financed by a grant from the FHNR tend to look after this upper section of the mountain, and have recently been doing excellent work in rehabilitating the upper trails from their degraded state.

Interesting to note that as long ago as 1998, it was suggested that a linking trail be made from the right-hand side of Protea, across to the upper section of Watsonia, in order to create an easier angled, non-slippery way up and down the mountain side. Over July / August 2022 the new Waboom trail was constructed, which gives a fine hiking trail from low on Watsonia, directly up into Disa gorge.

The Helderberg Nature Reserve goes from strength to strength. The HNR has been in the past, and remains to this day, greatly appreciated by the community.

References:
1970. Peggy Heap. The story of Hottentots Holland.
1998. Carol Purnell. A Management Plan for the Future of The Helderberg Nature Reserve.
Hayley-May Wittridge. Current Biodiversity Area Co-ordinator: Helderberg Nature Reserve.
Owen Wittridge. Current Biodiversity Area Co-ordinator: Steenbras Nature Reserve.

Helderberg Nature Reserve West Peak and the Dome

Fire in full spate across the south east face of the Helderberg Mountains from Driekop to West Peak. Saturday 11th June 2022.

At the time of my writing this, Saturday 23rd July 2022, we are in some ways still coming to grips with regard to the aftermath and damage to Helderberg Nature Reserve (HNR).

Over the 11th and 12th June 2022 a powerful wind born fire swept across the mountainside and broadsided into the HNR. Ironically this was immediately followed by two days rain of biblical proportions.

Within days City of Cape Town Biodiversity Management Team, who is responsible for HNR, were out assessing damage to infrastructure and trails, and I was privileged to be part of a small team that worked under HNR Management directions in order to survey the higher trails, their condition, and to report back.

We were all impressed with the clean-up work and the drive of HNR Mgt that didn't ask "how long shall we close the reserve", rather they asked, "How quickly may we allow the public back to enjoy the reserve."

Watsonia's stunning display from Watsonia trail HNR.

The author and well known local guide Andreas Gronevald begin to survey upper trail damage. Pic courtesy of Stu Summerfield

Nature however has seen it all before, and will see it again. Regeneration will come, and I sense a feeling of excitement from HNR staff and Andreas, as we wait see what the seasons post fire new life will bring, and how beautiful it will be.

A few months post both the 2010 and 2022 fires, high on Woodies trail young life returned amongst gaunt burnt out remains. Even the larger flora will come back within a few years.

Pics courtesy of Mick Dunwell

A little HNR Geology:

Lower and middle sections of the reserve are underlain by rocks of the Malmesbury Group approximately 900 million years old.

Specifically, within the Malmesbury Group the rocks in the lower reserve are part of the Tygerberg Formation, and consist of phyletic shales, siltstones and fine-grained greywackes.

These formations are often overlain by scree slopes resulting from erosion from the Table Mountain sandstone (some 400,000 years old) which make up the mountains of West Peak and the Dome. Over eons erosion and rock falls have created the talus (scree) slopes that skirts the upper mountain side.

Therein lies the cause of HNR's slippery jeep track – shales and siltstones when compacted become smooth and glassy when wet, and lend themselves to fast water runoff. Thus, clearing the already glassy section of any grit that may have supplied purchase.

Road tracks & trails

Helderberg Nature Reserve trails might be divided into three areas.
1/ Low level 'walks' that are confined within the 'Sugarbird' track.
- Red markers - Batis walk.
- White markers – White-eye walk
- Blue markers – Untitled walk.

2/ 'Trails' on the flank of the mountainside, laying between 'Sugarbird' and the high-level contour of 'Woodies' – so named after one of HNR's early conservators Mr Douglas Wood.

3/ The high mountain trails leading to West Peak and the Dome.

This guide is primarily concerned with 'high' issues, and as such we seek the quickest and more direct routes to the upper mountains.

As many habitués of HNR will tell you, the reserve's slippery jeep tracks are notorious for slips and falls; especially whilst negotiating the bends. No matter how much care you may take, there are not many people, including myself,

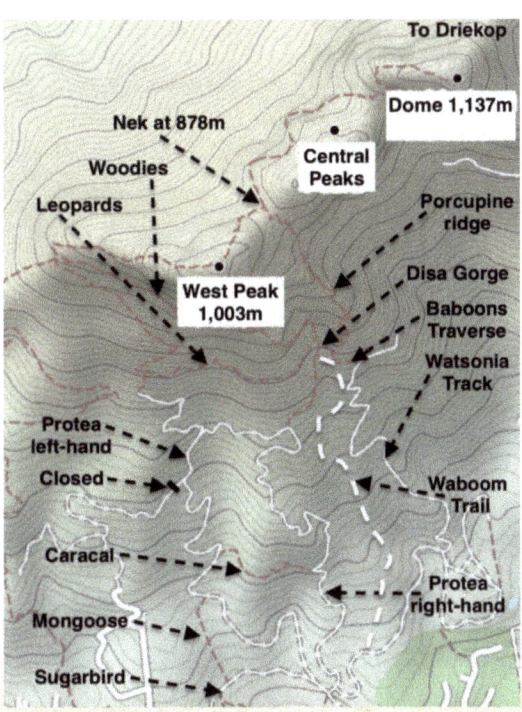

who have not at some time skidded and slipped with an undignified thump to find yourself unceremoniously dumped on your backside. Hopefully all you will suffer is a bruised ego, but folk have broken ankles and have had to be evacuated by the rescue services.

When damp many of us think twice about negotiating the jeep tracks. When it is raining……beware!

West Peak

Grade 3B Orange (3 out of 4 for effort, B for some exposure, Orange for some hands-on scrambling).

Often West Peak is the first top for the aspiring hikers who begin to turn their attention from the lower trails to the summits.

From the entrance to hikes under the big wooden beam by the car park, take a right and follow the trail through the delightful lower wooded part of the reserve - initial section of 'White eye trail – white markers.

After 200m you will reach the 'three tree ring' junction. Then pick up the 'Batis' trail immediately opposite – red markers - to climb gently up to reach the contour jeep track of Sugarbird. Now take a right for 40m before turning back left to climb the short cut of the Mongoose trail which leads you up to Protea left hand.

Follow this trail uphill for 1km to gain the steep left-hand turn which leads to the jeep track end. The journey now changes to a mountain trail as it climbs up to gain a series of zigzags which eventually lead to a long-left hand diagonal which meets the rather loose junction with the trail that climbs up on the left from Helderberg Plaas.

Now follow directions to the top of West Peak as written in the previous Helderberg Plaas Farm section of this guide.

Disa Gorge

Happy to say that Disa Gorge escaped the wrath of the June 2022 fire, such that all the original Disa Gorge signs remain in place. There are several areas within HNR that escaped the fire. These oases provide islands of protection for fauna, and from these 'safe havens' new life will move out to recolonise the reserve.

Post fire porcupines have already been seen digging for tubers and tortoises have been found foraging on the burnt ground. Boomslangs and Cape Cobras have also been seen repopulating the reserve.'

Fauna that did not survive the fire were quickly cleaned up by crows and birds of prey. Leopard prints were found high on West Peak only days after the fire. Nature has a way, sometimes harsh, but it works.

~~Leopard's Loop~~

Grade 2A Green
Three options may be used when approaching routes that radiate out from the lovely Disa gorge. The quickest way through the lower Sugarbird 'forest' area is the same for all, and that is to follow white 'White Eye' trail markers, turning right at the 'three tree circle then almost immediately back left to continue up 'White eye' to emerge from the lower forest at the Protea right-hand junction.

From where you then have three choices:
1/ Follow Protea right-hand up past the low-level contour trail of Caracal – ideal for a hiker or trail runner out for a short day - and on up to the right-hand Disa Gorge turn-off.
2/ Follows Protea right hand for just 10m before turning right onto Watsonia track to contour round for 300m until you pick up the new "Waboom" trail to your left – blue markers. This fine trail offers shade (when the bush regrows, as it surely will) and comprises great scenery and less slippery ground. A 'hikers trail' as opposed to a track, the upper Waboom traverses into Disa at the bridge. There is a right-hand upper link that ascends more directly to meet Baboon traverse exactly at the junction that leads up to Porcupine Ridge.
3/ You may of course continue up Watsonia until you reach the Baboon Traverse which is followed left to Disa. Add a further 20 minutes for this option.

A happy and experienced Gantouw club hiker poses in Disa Gorge at the Leopards Loop/ Woodies Walk junction.

It is worth noting that the last available water flows some 30m below the bridge. Above that point the stream disappears underground.

Rested at the bridge and having swopped greetings with other passing hikers, it is time to move on up the gorge. In the recent past there was a landslip that flowed down from just

below the start of Leopards Loop contour. This unstable ground led to the creation of a path ascending the right bank of the gorge – pink markers, crossing back left just above a large fallen tree. Please - this right hand (ascending) is the preferred trail as it avoids the loose ground and also avoids treading on tree roots that are susceptible to damage.
Either way, you will meet the sign pointing left to 'Leopards'.

Following the path, you suddenly emerge from the shade of the gorge to the light of the open mountainside. From here your labour is rewarded by enjoying the easy contour trail, whilst taking in the views that unfold. Track round the hill until you pick up the West Peak trail not far above the top of the jeep track.

Now take any combination of trails back down to the car park, though the fastest way down is to descend via Protea and the 'Mongoose' link trail.

Woodie's Walk **Grade 2.5A** Orange route – several rocky and steep sections.

After much TLC and hard work from HNR staff, Woodies was reopened in mid-September 2022.

Take the route to Disa Gorge as per Leopards Loop but then ascend the gorge for a further 40m to the sign pointing left to Woodies.

Please note that access to Disa above Woodies turn off is banned, due to the sensitive nature of the upper gorge flora, and due to a number of accidents – including a fatality - that occurred to folk trying to ascend the vertical very wet upper gorge.

With each gain in height the grade also rises, both in effort and techy 'hands on'. Woodies is no plain contour trail, as it climbs up and down following the skirts of the upper cliffs that gird the high reaches of West Peak. Soon after leaving the gorge the trail climbs past a copse of trees before descending gently to cross two gully outfalls. There are two 'down scrambles' which are straightforward, but the fire has stripped the hillside of fynbos bushes. This has had the effect of adding to the exposure, which some people may find disconcerting. The trail then becomes more straightforward as is crosses the hillside towards the junction with the clockwise West Peak trail.

Now follow the long downhill diagonal to reach the upper left-hand branch of Protea, as per 'Leopards Loop'.

West Peak **1,003m. Anti-clockwise** via Porcupine Buttress.
Grade 3B Orange+ Some rock scrambling. Four to five hours.

A mountain is like a woman. To be treated with love and respect in all its moods - which may be capricious and subject to sudden change. The higher up you go the more you may need hands on the mountain. Take weather into account; wind and rain will chill you and mist can hide the way! Never take a mountain for granted.

Heading up right from the bridge we climb out of Disa Gorge to take on the slope and buttress above. Alternatively follow the Waboom trail (a fine mountain path) and its right hand loop direct to a junction on Baboons traverse at the base of the Porcupine ridge trail Climb the zigzags upwards but please do not use or create any short cuts, whether you are racing, or just because you can. Using short cuts shows great disrespect for the mountain. During periods of rain these vertical cuts turn into erosion grooves that carry soil and stones down the mountainside, thus creating unsightly scars and damage to flora.

The route above looks improbable, but the trail follows a clever line of weakness.

Once you reach the cliff face, the trail steepens as it weaves its way left through cliffs and

The slightly airy gangway crossing to reach the final climb up to the nek. Leading is Hugh Middleton.

Looking across to West Peak from the summit of the Dome.

over rock steps. Expect some exposure. After 150m of ascent the angle eases back and the way leads past two more rock steps before heading horizontally right, taking in a narrow rock gangway before reaching the wide grassy slope that leads up to the nek.

We may not pass by West Peak without mentioning a well know character - Hugh Middleton. If you have ever been overtaken by an older hiker, going up or down, it is likely to be Hugh. As if climbing West Peak 165 times…and counting… was not enough, Hugh is also a font of hill craft and knowledge. In fact, the only way to get Hugh to slow down is to ask him a question. A ploy many of us have used, in order to get our breath back. I was present when Hugh's summit tally reached 100. I hope to be there to congratulate Hugh when he reaches 200.

The nek lies at a height of 878m, and is where we take a left to commit to the final scramble to the top. The route does not follow the north east ridge above you, but rather follows the easiest line which ascends its way up the mountains right-hand flank overlooking the R44 and Ekendal. The way can be tenuous and sketchy, even more so now that the fire has obliterated any signs of scuff and wear. There are plans to place new path indicators. Always best when first ascending to take a guide or go with an experienced hiker who knows the way.

The summit platform is complete with its concrete obelisk. Relax and take in the great views. Descend the south east ridge as previously described in the Helderbergplaas guide.

The Dome 1,137m

Grade 4C Red. A tough hike and a long day. Hands-on scrambling with exposure.
A fit hiking party may take 7 to 8 hours.

Climb to the nek as described in the West Peak guide via Porcupine Ridge, and pick up the trail that contours around the mountainside to your right.

Follow this trail round and up into the high maw of the Dome. The way above looks improbable but climb into the amphitheatre above and then ascend left up the steep trail that leads to the west ridge of the Dome. Now the angle lays back as the ascent passes through a large boulder field. Pass over several false tops until you reach the summit marker.

On descent great care is required, as it is very easy to descend too quickly on the north west flank. Many parties have had to re-ascend to the summit after finding their way down blocked by steep cliffs. Mark your ascent up the ridge very well in your mind, and carefully retrace your steps. As with West Peak, it is best to go first with a guide or hike group leader that knows the way.

Once back along the contour trail, descent from the nek at 878m is problematic. Then a very very careful descent is required down Porcupine ridge, as slips here have led to considerable tumbles and resulting injuries. Safer, though adding another hour to your hike, is the far longer option to climb up and over West Peak and down the other side.

A party traversing across the contour trail to The Dome. The ridge of Stellenboschberg in the background.

Perhaps better safe than sorry....

Driekop - the third `peak - 971m

The most remote summit on the Helderberg ridge section of the mountain rim, and the

Climbing up the final west ridge to the summit of the Dome.

third 'named' top.

Hard to grade, as it depends on the route chosen, but... as an extension to a Dome trip, it would take a fit hiker around ten hours round trip. Grade 5C Red. From Grootnek, assuming you may obtain permission from the owner of the estate at the head of the Paradyskloof valley, the ascent would still remain a good grade 4.5 C Red and would take around eight hours.
The route via the Dome and up from Grootnek is described in the 'Running the Rim'

Looking across from the Dome towards Driekop, Suurberg, Haelkop and Jonkershoek.

section of this guide.

~~Helderberg -~~ the Hidden Places

The following are well 'off the beaten track'. There are no trails to these places, and only a few know of their whereabouts. In a way it is counter intuitive to mention them at all; but interesting perhaps to think that though many know an area so well - there are still nooks and crannies that remain unknown to most. Access is frowned upon due to the environmental importance of sensitive fauna populations and entering these areas is considered intrusive to the unique species that survive there.

Bats Cave
Grade 5C Red

The short-exposed climb section has fall potential and rope is sometimes used on this 'difficult' step. One lady was on these moves when she froze and was heard to shout "I want a helicopter!" No route description. Just some tantalizing notes. The cave is quite deep with three vaulted sections, and is inhabited by several thousand Egyptian Fruit Bats. The floor of the cave oozes with thousands of years of bats pooh, and the occasional snake looking for a fallen youngster. Not to mention pathogens that are lying in wait just to cross species from bats to humans. Entry would be foolish, dangerous, and, covered in slimy pooh; you would also smell bad for some time.

Somewhere up there lie Bats Cave & Tokoloshe gorge

Beware of the bee's nest that is situated on the right wall of the cave. Too much noise brings them out to investigate. No, I'm not kidding.

Tokoloshe Gorge
Topography of course changes over time, even mountains come and go. At some time in the distant past the mountain slopes were of a quite different configuration. Perhaps much steeper and with greater precipitation. There certainly must have been a considerable flow of water to cut such a deep indent into admittedly an area of soft rock. We are left with a strange defile, quite short in length, that cleaves its way into the mountain slope. The lower section is fed by an almost continual spring, though the upper section is dry but still very slippery.

Suurberg 1,090m. Grade 3.5 B Red

An unsung orphan of the Hottentots Holland ridge set back as it is from the main chain, though well worthy of mention. Not high as many HH rim tops, but respected and only won by determination, as Suurberg has a long and difficult approach from any point.

Access is problematic, and must be obtained from the estate owners at the valley head.

Its south-west aspect viewed from Paradyskloof is of a continuously steep rocky mountainside. Our route lies right of this steep flank.

Once parked by the delightful letting cottage at the kloof end, take a left around the vineyard to pick up a trail that leads you to a wooded stream. Cross the stream to find your way up and left to find an easy to miss path that heads left up the hillside. Soon to join another trail to turn right and up to the flank of a gully reamed with huge boulders - looking like some giant's play pen. Pick your way carefully up this jumble for some 100m – it seems longer – until you reach a 20m long 3m wide obelisk that points upslope on the right of the jumble. At this point, exit the rock pile right, to find a faint trail that leads up the hillside to a nek.

Now take on the challenge of the ridge above by ascending diagonally left to find a cairned gully that leads back right through the rock bands which takes you up to ridge crest. Follow this undulating ridge until it is possible to contour round across a wet section of hillside to gain the flank of Suurberg. An unprepossessing top marked by a non-descript small pile of stones. Satisfying to get there though.

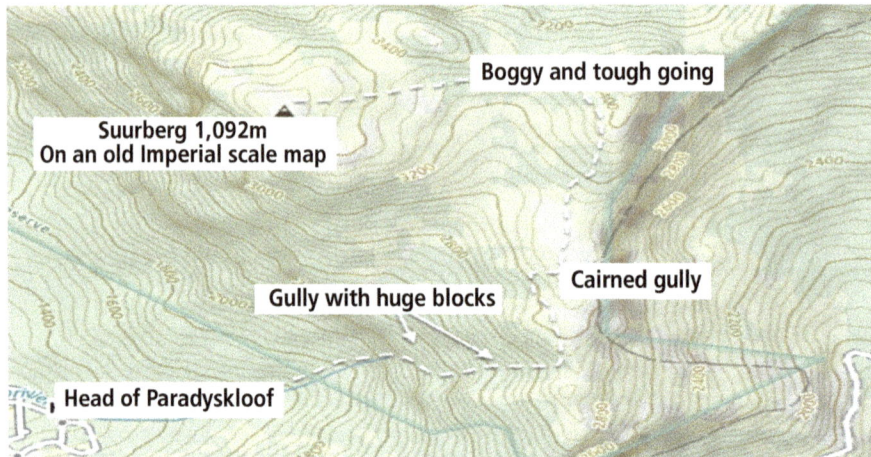

Haelkop 1,384m

An imperious mountain, and one that along with perhaps Hans se Kop is the shapeliest of all the mountains on the Helderberg Hottentots Holland mountain rim. It is hard won and not climbed that often.

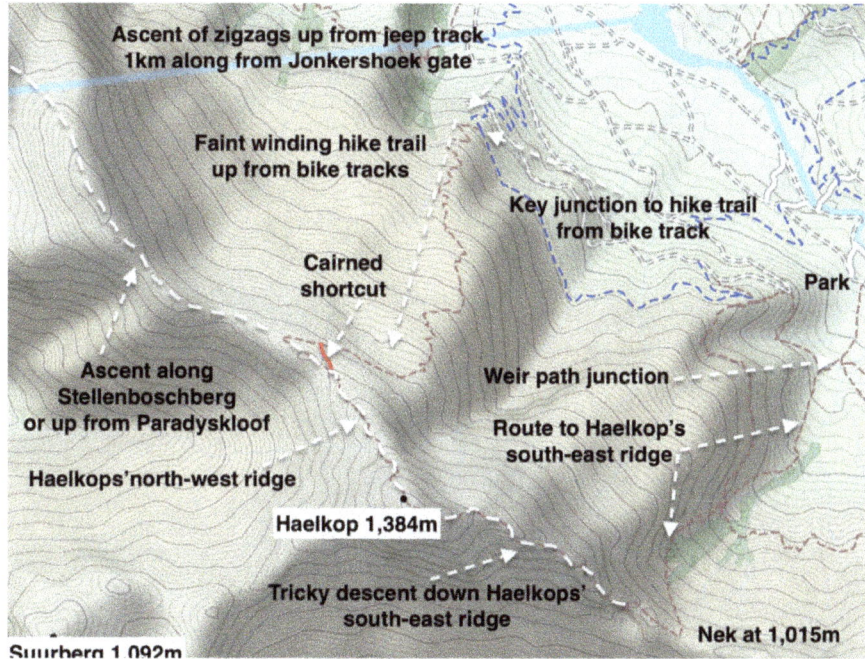

Haelkop mountain gives an impression of aloofness, and although not reaching the heights of Sneeukop or Victoria Peak, it feels like you are on a really isolated peak and one that is well worthy of respect.

Haelkops south east ridge Grade 4C Red
Much hand on scrambling, but never as bad as it looks.

Descending the ridge without first ascending it, is not recommended, as the way down appears quite intimidating and one continually feels the need to veer left, away from the ridge proper. This leads to much bruising bundu bashing. Once on this left flank, you tend to end up in one of the stream beds that leads down the mountainside. This is a very rocky area, and falls have occurred.

Ascending from the nek 1,015m towards the 'skeure' section of Haelkops south east ridge.

Looking back down Haelkops south east ridge from just right (east) of the ridge proper.

Taking in the ambiance whilst pausing on the scramble section of Haelkop's S/E ridge.

Getting past the tree. Possibly the crux scramble section.

Pic courtesy of Le Roux Kotze

Park opposite Cape Nature's Swartboskloof route sign after some 2km, having turned right along the Jonkershoek 'one way' ring road. Hike up and take the righthand fork at the small water works weir.

After some 100m look out for a trail turn on your left, cairned but easy to miss. Follow this up to the Sosyskloof contour trail. Follow this path right for some 40m to reach a trail leading diagonally back up to your left. Clear to follow at first, the trail becomes faint as it reaches the upper levels of a wooded kloof rising up from your left. We have cairned this trail at key sections, but losing the path is still possible . Worst comes to the worst; you are aiming for a drop in the ridge above and left. The trail wends its way left and up through a break in the cliff defences to reach the nek at 1,015m.

Now hike up towards the intimidating ridge above until you reach the first rock step. Traverse out to your right until it is possible to follow cairns to traverse back left onto the ridge. Now follow the ridge with slight deviations to the right. One of which passes by an old yellowwood tree - the crux scramble.

After climbing this steep corner to the nek, scramble right until it is possible to locate an easy passage down to the next nek. After which the ridge gives way to an easy passage to the summit.

There are further pics of this ridge in the 'Running the Rim' addendum at the back of this guide.

Haelkop north west ridge via Stellenboschberg Grade 5C Red

Trail runners can and have made the ascent right along Stellenboschberg ridge up Haelkop and back in one day; but for the hiker this may be a step to far. Many of us hike along the ridge of Stellenboschberg and then utilise a 'bivvy' (staying out overnight) at a point somewhere near the start of Haelkops north west ridge - though water can be an issue. This approach makes the morning ascent of Haelkop and its descent a far more manageable proposition.

Once on Haelkop ridge, follow the trail as it neatly picks its way up the least intimidating line to the summit.

Another overnighting approach is to climb out onto Stellenboschberg ridge by ascending up the steep trail from Paradyskloof. This is a shorter option, but would still be a grade 5 in effort if attempted in one day.

The author and Patrick Smit have reached the north west ridge.

Haelkop north west ridge from Jonkershoek Grade 4C Red

I should say that Haelkop is currently not one of Cape Natures 'allowed' hikes. We are trying to persuade CN to open up access. Thus, this description is put in for information.

Begin at the Jonkershoek gate entrance. I prefer early starts as it allows more time later in the day if things go wrong. Winter access - May, Jun, Jul, Aug, is 08:00 – 16:00. Summer - Sept, Oct, Nov, Dec, Jan, Feb, Mar, Apr, is 07:00 – 16:00

The trail up the intimidating ridge above 'goes' with little difficulty.

Hike in from the gate, taking the right hand one-way loop, to utilise a bridge that crosses the Jonkershoek river. Now look for a trail that heads up the mountainside using several zigzag turns. This is mountain bike territory and they are often on an unstoppable mission. If necessary, step off the trail in order to give them all the room they need.

At the bike route high point, look out for a hiker trail that heads up to your right. This is the start of the upper trail section that will lead you onto Haelkop north west ridge. It is faint in places, with several false trails, but it will lead you high up onto the flank of the mountain.

In its latter stage, the trail heads diagonally right up to the ridge……but look out for a cairned short cut which heads up left and crests the ridge at an old pylon base bypassing an unnecessary lower scramble. The summit now lies directly above you. Intimidating but not difficult.

Pic-Sans-Nom 1,184m

Grade 3+B Orange. 5 hours

View north west from the Triplet 1. Pic courtesy of Le Roux Kotze

The ridge from the nek 1,015m below Haelkop to Pic-Sans-Nom has been described in this guide's addendum section 'Running the rim'. So, we jump the intervening ridge and continue along the Hottentots Holland Rim, picking up at the next top, that of Pic-Sans-Nom.

This 'peak with no name' is also a seldom visited summit, though not due to its difficulty of approach, but more to do with its lack of being on many peoples' 'peak bagging' agenda. It is also usually missed off the 'tick list' of those running the rim, as it is a step too far, with a long way to go. So, it

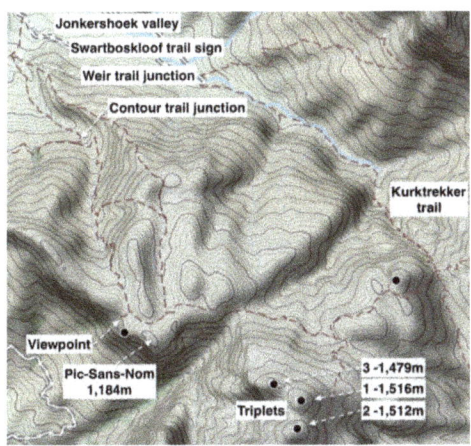

remains 'orphan like', on the periphery of desired peaks. Which is a shame as it holds great views of the area, as well as spectacular sights into the plunging depths of Diepgat.

Path junction with the way across to Sneeukop and the Landdroskop hut. The link now currently closed.

Distance wise the quickest approach is to begin as per the Haelkop south east ridge, by parking opposite Cape Nature's Swartboskloof route sign and hike up to the small water works weir, but this time we take a left turn at the weir to reach the contour trail in about one hour. Then take a left to make the long climb up the Swartboskloof, crossing the kloof outfall at a shady resting place before tackling the many zigzag sections leading to the nek at 1,100m. Many then make the 150m detour south west to take in the sudden fine view of the Helderberg basin far below. The summit of Pic-Sans-Nom lies but a short distance above to your left.

The Triplets No 1 – 1,515m No 2 – 1,503m, No 3 – 1,457m

Grade 4.5 C Orange. 7 hours for all three

Climbing Triplet 1, the highest, might leave this hike at a grade 4, but it's a long way to go

Looking across from the view point to Pic-San-Nom and the Triplets. Pic courtesy of Chris van Heever

Leonie and party enjoy the ambience of descending from T1 to T3. Pic courtesy of Le Roux Kotze

and not to climb them all, so the grade becomes 4.5.

To hike all three tops is a long day, necessitates hands on scrambling with much descent and ascent. A further note is that I have yet to see a map that does justice to the huge vertical drop that plunges down into Diepgat from the Triplets.

The quickest approach is to drive to the end of the Jonkershoek loop road to park by the Witbrug bridge. Then take the trail past the first and second waterfalls, and on up the degraded steep slope of Kurktrekker until it crests and reaches a trails crossroads. Straight ahead lies a much loved but currently closed - by cape Nature - link trail to Nuweberg via Boegoekloof.

Turning right we tackle more zigzags that tack up to reach a left turn off from the Swartboskloof trail. We now take this turn off, though it is currently closed by Cape Nature. This 'no entry' is a great pity as it is a fine linking path to Sneeukop and the Shamrock hut. It is doubly sad in that it is the route taken in the 1840's by Maclear's surveyors, tasked as they were with setting up the observation point atop Somerset Sneeukop, thus the trail has much historical significance. See the Somerset Sneeukop Maclear's story section of this guide.

Follow this trail until it is possible to strike off right to ascend Triplet 2. Though it's very steep northerly aspect means that you then have to retrace your steps until you may swing right – facing the mountain to contour onto the scree slopes that lie between T2 and T1.

Climbing T2 is often missed out due to its isolation and time-consuming ascent and descent. Many parties strike directly up to the nek between T2 and T1. The scree is arduous going and it is easier to take the slope on the right, leading to the summit of Triplets 1 at 1,515m.
The ridge down to T3 is very enjoyable, as it swings round with grand views and easy scrambling to pass by the abyss of Diepgat.

To descend; go down to reach the trail you used for ascent. Though some parties prefer to take the trail left to descend Swartboskloof, rather than descend the loose Kurktrekker.

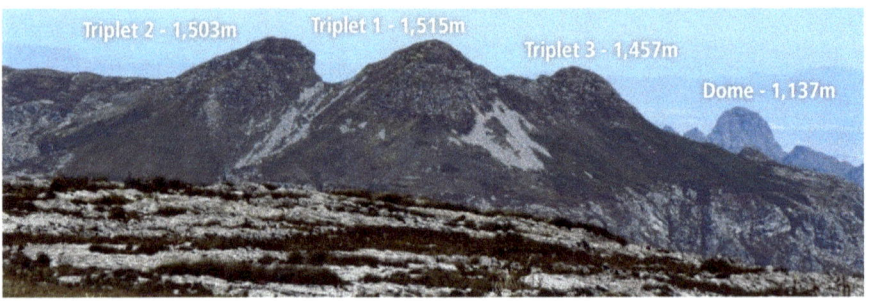

View looking west from Victoria Peak. Pic courtesy of Stu Summerfield

Somerset Sneeukop (Snow top) 1,590m

Sneeukop is the highest top we will reach on our Rim odyssey.

To me she is female, the queen of all the surrounding mountains. In winter she is sometimes seen wearing a crown of snow, thus further enhancing Sneeukop's beauty and superiority over her neighbours.

She is also, by one metre the highest summit in the Hottentots Holland range. Beating Victoria Peak at 1,589m by one solitary metre. Build a big enough cairn on the top of Victoria Peak, and you could easily raise its height to that above Sneeukop.

Sounds implausible, but this has actually been done in Scotland where the story goes that the lovers on one particular mountain were upset that their top was upstaged in height by another slightly higher mountain. So, taking the matter in hand they built a 4m high cairn on their mountain's summit to thus claim additional height. The claim was discounted, though the huge cairn on Scotland's Beinn Lair remains.

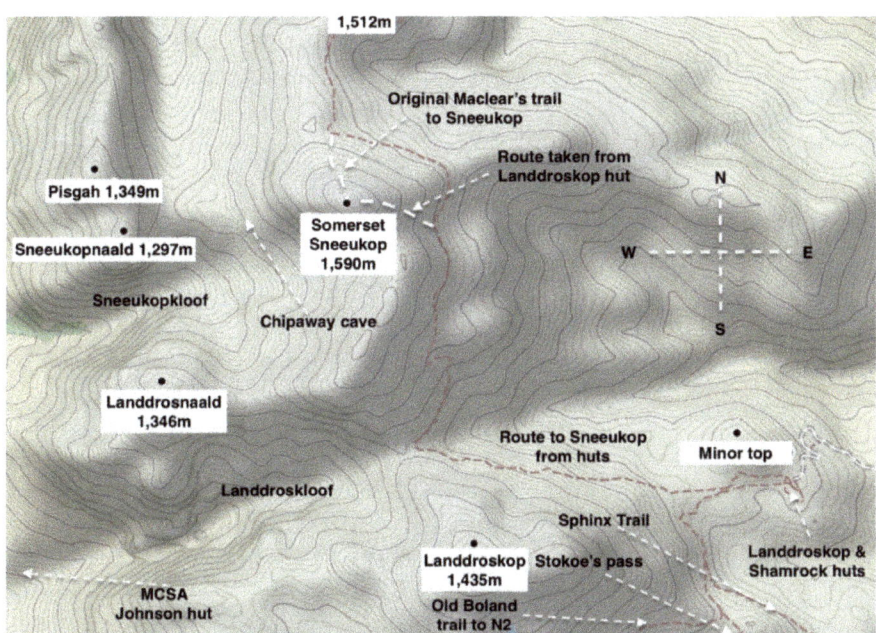

In fitting with her status, Sneeukop is a much sought after top, but she is one that not easily gained. The earliest recorded forays to its top was by men of Maclear's survey team, who made the arduous journey in all-weather from the road head at Jonkershoek, up Kurktrekker, past the Triplets and so on ascending to set up camp on Sneeukop's summit. Their amazing story is told in the next section of the guide.

Access to this prize is problematic, due to Cape Nature's ban on the use of all trails from the north, east and south and private land ownership for the all areas to the west. Thus, the following descriptions are written for posterity and with the fervent hope that this closure of our beloved trails will be reversed.

Sneeukop from the north – Maclear's surveyors' approach.

Grade 5B Orange. Nine hours.
Fit trail runners contemplate this route in a day. Grade 5 indicates that this route is off the scale. Assuming no overnighting, this approach and return, though not technical, makes for a very long day, and is only for the very fit and strong.

As per the Triplets description, park at the Witbrug bridge and take Kurktrekker up to follow the Swartboskloof trail anti clockwise until you reach the left turn which takes you past the Triplets. This section of the trail is 'currently' still in good condition due to its popular use pre ban.

After passing Triplet 2 the trail swings right - west - for 900m before turning south once more. Now the bulk of Sneeukop will fill the expanse in front of you. A further 900m takes you to another left turn in the trail. At this point look out for a faint trail that continues south up the blunt north flank of Sneeukop. In latter years this approach has fallen out of use in favour of staying at the Nuwerberg huts of Landdroskop or Shamrock, and tackling Sneeukop from there.

Contemplate as you take this route, how laborers carried heavy equipment up from

Hikers enjoy a summit break amidst the ruins of the old wall that protected Maclear's surveyors and equipment. Pic courtesy of David Wright

Jonkershoek to Sneeukop's summit. Though for them, it was a one-way trip as they slept out in the surveys summit tents.

Return the way you came, although given access, traversing on to the Nuwerberg huts is a more logical conclusion.

Sneeukop from the east – Via Nuwerberg Shamrock or Landdroskop huts.

Grade 3.5B Orange – from the huts - six hours round trip

Overnighting in one of the huts really takes the sting out of another otherwise very long approach. Pre booking via Cape Nature's booking system on 087 087 8250 is essential to obtain a place.

The hike to the huts via the jeep track will take roughly two hours. Conditions in the Landdroskop hut are basic but well appointed, with several dormitory rooms and a great central braai area. At the time it was possible to ask the authorities to take your 'stuff' including braai wood up to the hut. Last time I went, just pre Covid, this facility had been withdrawn, such that you had to carry all your equipment up with you. Best ask when you book as to what current rules apply.

Winter climb up the east flank of Sneeukop from the nek of Landdroskloof.

From the huts the trail is due west. At the time of writing, access to this trail is currently denied. We do not know why....as far as we are aware no hiker or hiking group was consulted when this ban was imposed.

Given access - this trail takes an amenable angle as it contours round the lower western flank of Landdroskop hillside, climbing slowly to reach a fine viewpoint at the nek of Landdroskloof. The trail now turns north and is gradually becoming overgrown due to lack of feet, though it is still discernible as it at first zigzags up before crossing several scree sections. The way now contours west around the easterly flank of Sneeukop, from where you must choose the best way to climb up the open hillside above. The options are several, and no one trail has been developed yet. Return the way you came.

Sneeukop from the west — Via Landdroskloof.

Grade 4B Orange – from the Johnson hut - 7 hours round trip.
Entry from the west side may only be facilitated by use of the Mountain Club of South Africa Johnson hut and by being a member of that organisation. Even then, hut entry must be pre-booked, and the intended route be logged with the estate concerned. The club has a procedure in place for this.

From the hut the climb up the lower Landdroskloof is through a pleasantly wooded shaded area. Take the right-hand bank at first, before crossing over at a hand wire guided ford to follow the left bank. You will soon pass the open area of the 'Koffiekloof' right hand turn. Ignore this option and continue ascending Landdroskloof. The upper section changes to an open aspect as the way climb directly up an unrelenting slope until you reach the nek in about three hours from the hut. Whence pick up the trail to Sneeukop as described above in 'Sneeukop from the east'.

Sneeukop from the west — Via Sneeukopkloof.

Grade 4B+ Red – from the huts a 7 1/2 hours round trip. Access rules as per Landdroskop. Graded slightly higher than Landdroskop due to the continuous scrambling nature of the lower section of the kloof. Not difficult but requiring much hands on climbing over blocks and past mini waterfalls, with slippery fall potential.

Ascending from the Johnson hut, after 40m take the left turn to cross the stream by the delightful summer dip pool. The trail continues steeply uphill to gain the jeep track which is followed as it contours round the hillside until it reaches Sneeukopkloof.

Cross the outfall to pick up a faint trail right which climbs up into the bush quite high on the left-hand bank of the stream. After some 500m you will eventually be forced by the steep banks into the stream bed itself. There are occasional options to climb the right bank, but after several ascents I think the stream bed is the easiest alternative.

Once out onto the open hillside, climb up to the kloof nek. Sneeukop's summit is now happily not far to your left, but still requires a 300m climb.

Descend the same way, or easier, traverse right (south) to descend Landdroskloof nek.
Your trip could be broken by an atmospheric night out in Chippaway cave. Location described elsewhere in the guide.

Looking across from above Chippaway towards the top right of Sneeukopkloof.

A dawn photo courtesy of Bennie de Beer showing left to right Sneeukop, the nek of Landdroskloof and Valleiberg, also a fine way to end this Sneeukop section.

Maclear's Beacon on Sneeukop summit - 1,590m

Between 1750 and 1753 the Frenchman Abbot Nicolas La Caille arrived in Cape Town with the avowed intent of measuring the shape of the southern hemisphere. At the completion of his 'Arc of Meridian' calculations, La Caille came to the conclusion that our planet had a somewhat flatter southern hemisphere and was therefore – 'pear shaped'.

However, it was thought by some, notably George Everest, Surveyor General for India at the time, that La Caille's measurements may have been affected by the gravitational pull of the mass of Table Mountain itself.

Thomas Maclear was an Irish-born medical doctor and keen astronomer, and it was to Maclear that the Admiralty turned in order to solve this enigma one way or the other. Thus, armed with a budget of £1,000 per year, Maclear set sail and arrived in Cape Town on 5 January 1834 and began work.

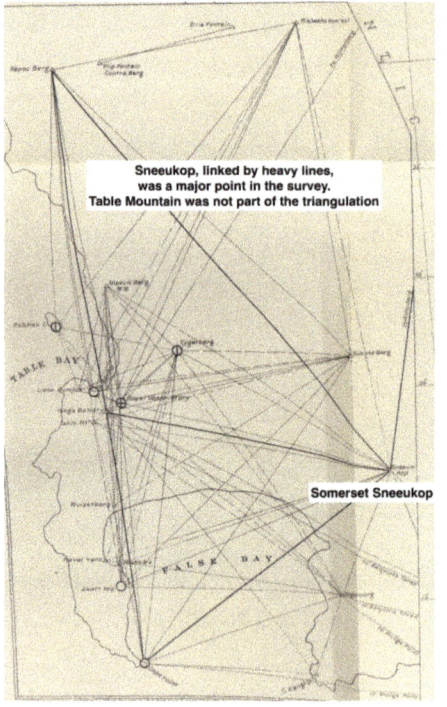

Sneeukop, linked by heavy lines, was a major point in the survey. Table Mountain was not part of the triangulation

In the decade that followed, Maclear and his associates carried out detailed surveys, placing measurement beacons on summits from Kamiesberg in the north, to Cape Point and Cape Agulhas in the south, Kimberley in the north-east and beyond Cape St Francis in the south-east.

Maclear was made a Fellow of the Royal Society of Astronomers and served as Her Majesty's Astronomer and Director at the Royal Observatory at the Cape of Good Hope from 1833 to 1870. He was knighted in 1860 for his achievements in astronomy. Sir Thomas Maclear was awarded the Queen's Medal in 1869. He has a crater on the moon and also a town in the Eastern Cape province of South Africa near the Mooi River, named after him, though I understand the town's name is now officially Nqanqarhu. He died in 1879 in Mowbray, Cape Town.

Table Mountain hosts the most well-known of Maclear's beacons. Unfortunately – and a little-known fact – Table Mountain's beacon was purely a 'passive' observation station. No theodolites were taken onto Table Mountain to measure the angles in the triangulation process. It is also clear that Maclear never visited the Table Mountain or the Somerset Sneeukop site.

The five points closest to Cape Town used in the triangulation survey were, in order of proximity to Cape Town: King's Battery, Cape Point, Somerset Sneeukop, Kapokberg and Riebeek Kasteel.

History of the Somerset Sneeukop Beacon

As assistant to Maclear, Charles Piazzi Smyth was tasked with setting up a beacon on the summit of Somerset Sneeukop. This position would be a major link in the triangulation chain.

Charles Piazzi Smyth

Piazzi, as he was known, was apparently of robust build. It was a strength that he would need for his time on Sneeukop.

In his later years, Piazzi would recall that *'the time spent on Sneeukop was probably the most trying of my life.'*

After his labours organising the erection of the Winterberg beacon, and following discussions with Maclear, Piazzi was assigned to erect a triangulation beacon on Somerset Sneeukop.

Two options were considered for the approach to Sneeukop: either from the north-west along and up from the Jonkershoek Valley, or from the south-west up the Lourens River. The fact that the south-west approach was considered at all is amazing, given the difficulty of any ascent up Diepgat, Sneeukopkloof or Landdroskloof, much respected hikes for any modern-day hiker.

Happily for us, Piazza kept a meticulous log of his activities, and on 3 November 1844 he was able to inform Maclear that *'I have at last the pleasure of addressing you from a new mountain….the first load is halfway up the mountain, and will probably be on the station tomorrow.'*

It is worthwhile noting with respect the considerable effort put in by labourers carrying tents, supplies and equipment on their backs.

The instrument and stand in five boxes weighed 1042 lbs (473 kg), with the heaviest case containing the body of the theodolite [which] weighed 400 lbs (181 kg). This last item had to be pulled and manhandled by several men using ropes.

In those days there were no paths, only a hard-going bundu bash that after many weeks changed into what could be loosely called an early trail – one that we enjoy today. Nor could they choose a nice day; the food and equipment had to reach the top to supply those making observations on the summit.

Todays hikers toil up Kurktrekker.

At the top of the long Kurktrekker haul the way turns right along what we call the Swartboskloof trail, until reaching the junction to turn left on the Jonkershoek traverse that leads along and down to the Landroskop hut.

Traversing along the south-east slopes of The Triplets the struggling men reached an indent at 1,463m, before finally ascending the blunt north ridge to gain the summit of Somerset Sneeukop at the height of 1,590m.

Even today this is a challenging hike, sadly currently out of bounds as Cape Nature has closed this historic path. We entreat the authorities to reopen this classic link trail that joins Nuweberg and Jonkershoek - a trail created in such historic circumstances.

The station on Sneeukop, Hottentots-Holland. Sketch by C. Piazzi Smyth, 1842. Note tent protecting transit instrument.

– *Courtesy of Africana Museum, Johannesburg*

There followed a hiatus in activities on Sneeukop, while equipment was brought from other triangulation summits. However, by 7 December 1844 Piazzi was established on the summit. One tent housed the labourers and Piazzi, the other housed the instruments.

Writes Piazzi: '[T]he thermometer registers in the daytime between 40 (4.5C) and 50 (10C)….misty days are the rule and not the exception.

18th Dec – *a 1/4inch (0.6cm) of hoar frost.*

7th Jan – *temp 37.5 (4degC).*

3rd Feb – *two of our marquees (large tents) were torn to shreds by the north east wind.*

27th Mar – *Heavy rains, which at least restored our water supply.'*
The observations continued….

16th May – *mist and sleet… one could not stand up before the wind.*

17th May — *the last loaf was eaten. We set off down for rations, though the paths were slippery with ice and snow: the waterfalls of course very fine.*

21st May – *Barwise and Frederick started up with supplies. The rain came down heavily and continued for three days.*
At 5hr P.M violent wind and rain. Barwise arrived without Frederick. Barwise and Stoffel went to look for Frederick, returning on 20 minutes ….without trace of Frederick.

22nd May – *Raining and blowing. A, B and S again set out to search, again without success.*

23rd May – *Bell tent blew over.*

25th May – *There could be no doubt that the unfortunate man was dead… B was taking matters coolly and said there was no use in further searching. I told B that F's death lay at his (B's) door, for allowing him (F) to become drunk that night, and by letting F carry up 3 times the load as heavy as his own………. that he (B) should do nothing but look for the corpse; that if he attempted to leave the place before that was done, he would be taken up by the police on suspicion of murder.*

26th May – *B started off early this morning on search, in a tremendous fright came back at 10 AM saying that he had found the body.*
I went down with A, B & S to the place where the body as lying. Only 1/10th of the whole distance away from the tents. With all the major difficulties behind.
We climbed down S.S.E for 500 yards (450m), down a sloping boggy kloof where we found the body lying on its back as if asleep; the bag of rations still on, the hands folded across the breast and stuck in the cuffs of the opposite sleeve, the legs stretched out close together. He might have gone down for shelter: but could get no further…..for there the kloof breaks down suddenly into a precipice.
B was made to cover up the body with a piece of canvas. The body was frozen.

29th May – *Stoffel and Adonis started up with urgent rations, but when they were half-way up, the icy wind met them so violently, combined with snow, they were deprived of all feeling in their hands and feet, they thought it prudent to retreat.*

5th Jun – *Tent sheets covered with ice up to ½ inch. Unable to break tent open, the (canvas) door had to be melted with boiling water.'*

It would appear to have been an unusually savage autumn.

With bad weather seeming set for several days, Piazza set off down to the Cape Town Observatory. It was his first respite from the mountain since October the previous year. He was greatly heartened to find a letter which announced that he was to succeed Thomas Henderson as Astronomer Royal for Scotland.

Piazza was expected to take the next passage back to the UK, but volunteered first to complete the Sneeukop observations. Finally, on 28 August, despite the evacuation being delayed by many days of snow, the last loads were brought down off the mountain.

Like many mountaineers, I have spent days, weeks, even months whilst on expeditions living in tents and surviving bad weather; but we had modern equipment.
The extreme conditions which the surveyors and their labourers had to survive was truly remarkable, one man even paying with his life.

Footnote:
La Caille was trying to determine the radius of curvature of the Earth in the southern hemisphere and compare it with the radius in the northern hemisphere – not the circumference. Unbeknown to La Caille the attraction of gravity caused by the mountain masses of Table Mountain and the Picketberg range near Aurora affected his observation hence the anomalous calculations.

We may note that it was not the magnetic attraction of the mountains that affected the observations but rather the gravitational attraction that was the main cause of the anomaly. From his observations, Maclear was able to prove that indeed, the shape of the southern hemisphere of the earth is the same as the northern.

If you sit in a restaurant drinking a glass of wine or a cup of coffee next to Table Mountain, the surface of your beverage will be tilting imperceptibly towards the hillside as it is pulled by the mountain's gravitational mass.

References:
1/ Richard Wannacott – Personal correspondence. Retired Director of Survey Services (within the Chief Directorate: National Geospatial Information), and former Global Navigation Satellite Systems Consultant at Umvoto Africa on borehole monitoring and mapping.

2/ Warner, Brian (1983). Charles Piazzi Smyth, Astronomer-Artist, his Cape years 1835 - 1845. Cape Town: A.A.Balkema. Published for UCT.

3/ http://assa.saao.ac.za/sections/history/astronomers/smythe_cp/

Outriders of Sneeukop

Pisgah and Sneeukopnaald

Access can only be gained by obtaining 'approach' permission from the estates on the west of the rim, plus an opening up of Cape Nature's access for the western kloofs. See Sneeukop map.

Pisgah 1,349m. 3.5 B Orange. Derived from the Hebrew word for summit.

Graded as for an ascent from the Johnson hut.

A problematic approach befitting the summit of a lonely, inaccessible, and rarely visited mountain.

On it's north west face Pisgah sports the steepest aspect of any mountain face on the Helderberg / Hottentots Mountain Rim, with its sheer face dropping down for over 450m to the right flank of Diepgat. See the rock-climbing section of this guide.

Hike across to the entrance of Diepgat, which is ascended via its rocky steps (described in the Diepgat guide section) and turning right ascend the Staircase until you reach the Sneeukopnaald / Staircase nek. Thence ascend west upslope to the nek between Sneeukopnaald and Pisgah. Scramble up right to reach Pisgah's summit.

Alternatively and somewhat easier, ascend Sneeukopkloof turning left to reach the same nek as described above.

Sneeukopnaald — Sneeukops 'needle' - 1,297m. 3.5 B Red
Use the same alternative approaches as for Pisgah. Sneeukopnaald is separated from Pisgah by 300m and a nek between them that necessitates hiking down 180m from Pisgah then make an exposed traverse left across a grass rake to gain a rock band which bars the way forward. Scramble up the rock step, easiest on the right to gain the final summit cone. Very few will have come this way before you!

Pic courtesy of Stu Summerfield

Landdroskop 1,435m 3.5B Orange.

See the Sneeukop map.

Access difficulties as discussed, apply to this route.

This substantial peak may be ascended from the Johnson hut via the long haul up Landdroskloof to the nek and take a right turn as per the topo picture.

Alternatively stay a night at the Landdroskop hut and ascend as per the easterly approach to Somerset Sneeukop; taking a left at the nek of Landdroskop kloof.

Landdroskop may also be ascended as part of navigating the marathon of the Hottentots Holland rim.

Looking up the North west ridge of Landdroskop 1,435 m from Landdroskloof nek. Pic courtesy of Stu Summerfield

Valleiberg, Langklippiek & Langkloofberg

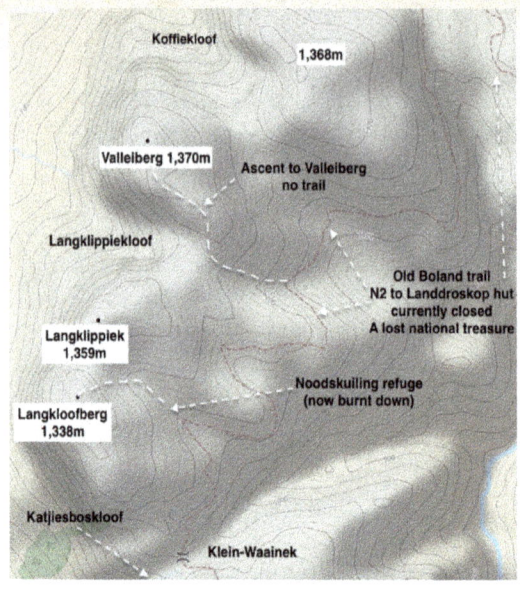

There are no trails for the final sections of the following ascents, and access permission would need to be obtained from the estates concerned and from Cape Nature regarding all of the routes noted below.

We are now entering an area of very remote peaks, accessible only by staying out overnight, or by determined fit trail runners!

All three peaks have problematic approaches, such that I am going to assume that they will only be considered by experienced strong hikers that are equipped and are used to carrying and using overnighting gear. Also, that they are also prepared for whatever the weather may throw at them. Such that they can weigh the logistics required for what-ever approach they decide to use.

Accompanied by experienced friends, I have trekked into this remote area and have spent the night out, ready to snatch a summit the next day. A clear evening can give way to a stiff cold south-easter, bringing with it boiling cloud that billows around you; quickly turning reality into only so much as you can reach out and touch. Everything else beyond a few meters becomes lost in a chilling opaque grey damp fog. Be prepared to be able to find your way down in such conditions!

Valleiberg Johnson hut via Koffiekloof and Crystal Ridge
Grade 3D (very exposed) **Black** (serious scrambling).

First written up in a 1965 'Explosives and Chemical Industries' magazine article. This scramble has been lost to time, and it is now thought possible that rockfall has rendered this approach anything other than a serious undertaking. Several attempts have been made to repeat the route with no success to date. Should only be attempted by an experienced roped party.

From the Johnson hut, continue up Landdroskloof until the kloof opens out and it is possible to turn right into Koffiekloof. Once a cairned trail, now much overgrown, I did come across several old cairns in my own forays up this kloof to the waterfall.

Skirt the waterfall on the right to re-enter the kloof and scramble up for a further 180m. Thence turn right and climb out onto the ridge and follow this until it meets the rock of the upper section of the mountain. Then traverse right to a 'loose' gully which splits this section of the mountain; follow this to its crest. The summit now lies but a short distance to your right.

Valleiberg from the east.
Grade 1.5B Orange. Graded only for the final section from the 'Old Boland Trail to summit'. It will be a grade 4 hike just to get to this start.

Assuming you have stayed out overnight on the east side of Valleiberg in the vicinity of the old Boland trail, ascend north-west via the gully or blunt spur to its right. This will take you to where you are able to look down Langklippiekloof - see map above. A further 240m climb up the reasonable north west spur above will take you to the top.

Descent could be by any of several very long exits via the old Boland trail to the N2, Stokoe's pass down to Grabouw, or to Nuwerberg via the Sphinx trail. Alternatively descend Langklippiekloof and swing north below the west face of Valleiberg to regain the Johnson hut.

Langklippiek & Langkloofberg
Grade 1B Orange. Graded only for the final section from the 'Old Boland Trail to the two summits. Again, it will be a grade 4 hike just to get to the old Nordskuiling refuge start.

On the Helderberg basin side, the kloofs, Langklippiekloof and Katjiesboskloof left hand that flank these two mountains are both reasonable in ascent and descent. In ascent the heavily wooded area of Langklippiekloof should be avoided as far as possible by keeping well to the right side of the kloof. In its upper section the kloof forks though the best line is obvious, finishing in a long section of loose stone 'moraine'. The alternative branch is not easy as a short waterfall would have to be negotiated.

Overnighting, as I have done, it is possible to 'doss' down' in the now burnt down Noodskuiling refuge, as the concrete floor is still useable. There is a resident grumpy Berg Adder!

A small figure in red is approaching the refuge just above centre of the picture.

For Langkloofberg, climb left up the slope above the refuge, taking in a few minor rock steps.

For Langklippiek descend north to the nek between the two tops and hike up easy ground to its summit.

Then, as for Valleiberg, choose your way out.

Settling down on the floor of the old 'Noodskuling' refuge. Pic courtesy of Stu Summerfield

Summit of Langkloofberg with False Bay on the left and West Peak/Dome beyond.

Within this section of the guide lies the most complicated area of the entire Hottentots Holland Mountain Rim

Diepgat to Sneeukopkloof

Gazing up from anywhere within the Helderberg basin, you might be forgiven for thinking that the rim is made up of one continuous line of peaks and neks. However, between Diepgat and Sneeukopkloof lie two separate mountain ridges that completely hide a secluded valley that nestles between them. The 'Staircase' (Trappieskloof) as this 'lost valley' is known, is seldom visited. Only the very intrepid ever get to see this wild place.

At the base of the 'Staircase' lies Trappieskloof, which is the name of the kloof that makes a sharp right turn away from Diepgat to make its own solitary way up between the mountains, though the tumbling mountain stream soon peters out to become an open wide slope.

Looking south on the approach to Diepgat Peaks of Landdrosnaald, Valleiberg and Langklipeik to the right. The conclusion of the 'Rim' may be seen above Gordons Bay on the far right.

The 'Staircase' is made up on its right by the ridge of Pisgah – 1,349m to Sneeukopnaald - 1,297m, whilst the towering mass of Somerset Sneeukop – 1,590m lies on the left.

Diepgat - A grade 4.5C Red hike, possible in one tough day including your walk out.

Please be aware that the exit trail from Somerset Sneeukop to Landdroskop and Shamrock lodge huts is currently closed by Cape Nature. We hope that this barred access is temporary, as it is a much-loved trail. Your only logical option is to descend the Swartboskloof trail down into Jonkershoek.

Access: Members of the MCSA may ask the club for permission. The club in turn will apply to Lourensford Estate.

Usually spelt in two words 'Diep Gat'. The phrase is solid Afrikaans and its pronunciation to the English reader is not obvious as I know to my cost as I have been picked up several times by locals regarding my incorrect intonation. The 'Diep' is shortened to 'Dip', whilst the 'G' in 'Gat' is pronounced with a German like guttural like rolling 'gh'. The 'a' is also shortened to be almost a quick 'u'. Only the 't' remains a 't', to give respite to the none Afrikaans speaker. Its literal translation is descriptively - 'Deep Hole'.

Diepgat is the most savagely deep kloof and arguably the most impressive that transcends the Hottentots Holland Rim. The kloof finally tops out at 1,090m, with the Jonkershoek Swartboskloof trail just a stone's throw away.

Whilst Diepgat is not technically difficult, much of the way follows the Diepgat stream with almost continuous boulder hopping. Such that any ascent is best left to dryer periods, otherwise it remains slippery and dangerous in ascent or descent. Fallen trees also add to your logistical difficulties.

Interestingly the Lourensford river is the fastest flowing shortest perennial river in South Africa. The original European name for the river was the Tweederivier, as it was the second river crossed after the "Eersterivier" on the journey from the Cape Peninsula. The name was changed to the Lourensrivier in honour of one - corporal Lourens Visser, who drowned in the river.

The Trail:
Leaving the last trace of the jeep track at the bend just before it crosses the Lourensrivier, the way climbs on the left bank of the river, passing by the ruins of old cycle bridges that were built for the mountain bike EPIC event. Startling to see how quickly natures claims back its own, as the wooden slats are rotting and are being covered by undergrowth.

A flat area known as 'Picnic Bush' is soon reached on your left. This is an historic site, being used by both the Khoekhoe and later European settlers.

Shards of pottery found at the site have been designated by academia as belonging to the Khoekhoe period, which makes them between 2,000 to 250 years old.

Looking up the lower section of Diepgat, shortly after leaving the historic 'picnic bush'. Pisgah North wall on the right and summit of Pic-Sans-Nom on the left.

For approximately 150 years this flat area high up the mountain slope was used by early settlers, who would gather together at 'Picnic Bush' to celebrate Christmas and Easter.

There is no trail within the Diepgat kloof, apart from the riverbed itself, and this is where you must go. Unremitting boulder hopping and climbing over tree obstacles, with every possibility of a slip and consequent damage to ankle or leg. Care definitely required.

After roughly an hour and a half after leaving 'Picnic Bush', depending on water levels, you will reach 'Jocks Camp'. We do not know the history of this site, but it is believed to have been built by an early MCSA member as a base from which to explore the area. The walls and door opening still stand in memory of someone who was very determined to build a refuge in a high remote place. If you were to begin your ascent late in the day, this would be an ideal place to stay for the night.

Lower Diepgat 'Jocks camp'.

A further five hours river ramble should see you at a second old, smaller and much overgrown refuge – again on the left side of the river. A forlorn old rusting braai grill hangs from a nearby branch. It has probably hung there for over a decade or three.

The awkward scramble bypass before meeting Diepgat/Trappieskloof junction. In dry weather it may be easier to climb the waterfall.

Having no hard data, it may well be that this site is 'Jocks Camp'.

Not long after leaving this high camp you will reach the only real obstacle which may bar your way up Diepgat. A small waterfall is reached, impassable in all but low water, there is a bypass by climbing a slippery wall on the left, utilising tree roots to gain a higher way through. Fall potential of 4 to 5 meters.

H. V. Bagley, writes of this section in the MCSA journal of 1917, that we *'encountered the only troublesome pitch, although this did not offer very great difficulties.'*

Further easing scrambling soon leads you out of the trees and onto the unrelenting open slopes above. A further two hours of sweat from the junction scramble should see you at the nek.

Diepgat cave
This remote cave lies high on the left flank of Diepgat.

Looking down Diepgat, you will see a line of three scree beds. At the lower of the three scree slopes, where the scree bed tails off to a point, begin to traverse left (north)

There are two small scrambles to be overcome before reaching the cave shown by the arrow.

Diepgat / Staircase / Chippaway cave / Sneeukopkloof circuit

Grade 5C red. 9 hrs. This is a big hike, so best done in two days.

One option is to start late, maybe after finishing work on a Friday, and spend the night in the lower Jock's camp, it may then be possible to complete the remaining circuit on the following day.

Traverse across to Diepgat cave.

A more satisfying excursion is to make it to Chipaway cave on energetic day one. Then descend Sneeukopkloof on day two. With either option, be aware that this a tough hike, off trail, and one in which each member of the hike should be experienced

Shortly after the waterfall left hand by-pass as noted in the Diepgat ascent description, the kloof opens out enabling you to see the dip on the right-hand skyline that shows line of Trappies (staircase) kloof. Head up this right-hand branch outfall.

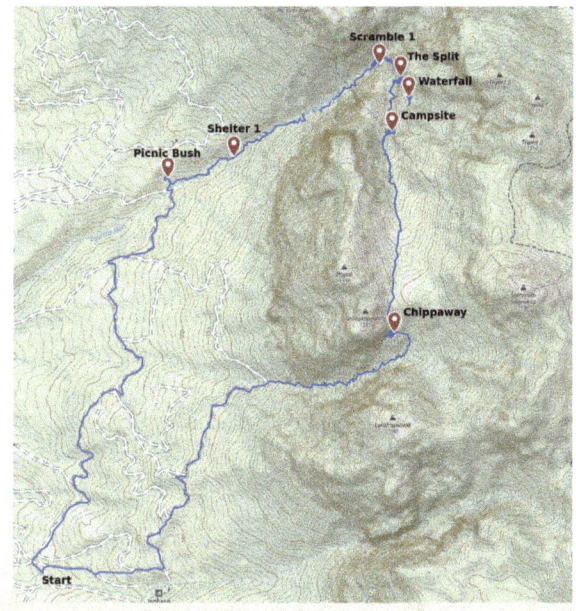

Route shown - Johnson hut/Diepgat/Staircase/ Chipway Cave/ Sneeukopkloof/Johnson hut

Shortly after turning into Trappieskloof, a fork in the stream is reached.

If you take the left-hand outfall, you will after 30 minutes of easy scrambling reach a fine cascade down a steep mossy emerald green rockface. It is possible to scramble further up and right, but the way becomes steep and the rocks unstable, with a real danger of causing loose stones to fall on those below you.

Unless you really wish to view the emerald wall, take the right-hand scramble as shown in the photo. Cross the stream and climb up the bank above, to reach a rock face. Now follow a traverse left to reach easier ground as the valley gradually opens out before you.

A dead end lower left turn up from Trappiesskloof.

Junction with waterfall dead end on the left, Trappieskloof on the right. Climb over the obvious blocks and then ascend the right wall to gain a traverse left. Most awkward section of Trappieskloof ascent.

The way gradually climbs out of the wooded lower section and gains more open slopes above. All the way up to the Nek at 1,196m the ascent remains easiest by following the right flank. If time is a problem, it would be possible to rough camp on the relenting slope, as some previous parties have done. But the prize is to push on and experience history by joining the select group that has overnighted in Chipaway cave. It should take roughly four hours to climb up from Diepgat to the Nek at the top of the Staircase. From here you are able to view down into Sneeukopkloof. However, your sleepover spot lies still further up the hillside…..but not far.

From the nek at the top of the Staircase climb up and left, looking out for the prominent finger of rock on the left.

Looking down Trappieskloof having just left the wooded lower section. A subsiduary kloof left of Diepgat 'Nuwejaarskloof' lies to the right of the Pic' Ridge leading to Pic-sans-nom above.

Ascending the upper section of the 'Staircase'. Nuwejaarskloof left of centre.

No one knows when this cave was first visited and slept in, but its history goes way back to the early days of the Mountain Club of South Africa. There is a metal tube containing 1st aid items that must be decades old.

Time and effort have been spent building a wall to break the wind, and to make the refuge reasonably weather tight.

Reaching Chippaway refuge, high and left up Sneeukopkloof.

Savour this place, and the unique mountain experience it will give you.

The cave sleeps four. More if they are super friendly. The outside balcony may be preferable in good weather, where there is room for another three or four.

Descent: The way now is below you, though you have the option of climbing out of Sneeukopkloof and ascending Somerset Sneeukopkloof, which in truth is not far above you.
The descent offers no technical difficulties, though continued concentration is required as you negotiate the never-ending rocky descent.

In the past I have cairned the easiest line,

Route to Chippaway cave upper right side of Sneeukopkloof.

Chippaway Cave Pic courtesy of Nico van watt

Room with a wild view.

though winter torrents may have dislodged some cairns.

Three hours should see you back in the Johnson hut, after having spent an exciting time on the wild side.

All photos in the Diepgat and Chipaway cave – courtesy of Dante Visser

Katjiesbokloof

Continuing our sojourn right, after the summit of Langkloofberg, the skyline drops down to take in Katjiebokloof

Katjiesbokloof - Small Cat's Gully. Grade 3.B Orange. If you stay the night.

To enter the kloof from below, depending on your point of egress, you will need the permission of Idiom, Wedderwill Game Park, Vergelegen Estate, or a combination of all three. Any approach to this area is going to be tough, with no trails, thick fynbos on rocky terrain! H. V. Begley and party recorded an ascent 1917, with no further 'recorded' ascents until 1998. The outcome of our more recent explorations is that although it is stated that Katjiesbokloof was ascended in 1917, it is thought that this ascent was made up the 'Katjiesbokloof Left Hand' (KLH). Katjiesbokloof 'proper' is barred in its lower reaches by extensive waterfalls.

Approach KLH on its right-hand side until you can line up three large flat boulders, as per the arrow showing 'Cairned entrance'. From here it is possible to follow our cairns through this delightful 'enchanted forest', at first horizontally for some 80m, before following the cairns up-hill to the steeper finish just before the cave. This abode will sleep four and the view is stupendous.

Typical lower gully scenery *Cave accommodation with a view!*

From the cave, track back left to the kloof and make your way up through trees that must have thankfully survived many centuries of fires. This is a special place, visited by only a handful of people.

Water, if it is there at all has disappeared underground - carry up what you need.
The climb now breaks out of the trees to take in patches of scree before reaching a final steepening grass slope that takes you out to just up and left of the top of Katjiesboskloof proper - Klein-Waainek - with the Boland trail awaiting below you.
A number of tough exits exist.

1/ Back the way you came. A further four to five hours of tough going.
2/ Take a right to head out along the old Boland Trail to the N2. A five hour hike out, but at least on a trail, and water available by the trail as it contours the southern face of Moordenaarskop.
3/ Take a left and make the equally long five-hour hike to the Landroskop hut. There is usually water in the stream as you cross Guinevere's field. From the huts you also face another 1.5 hour walk out down the Sphinx trail or the jeep track to Nuwerberg.

Moordenaarskop and Hans se Kop

Moordenaarskop - Murderers Peak – 1,340m

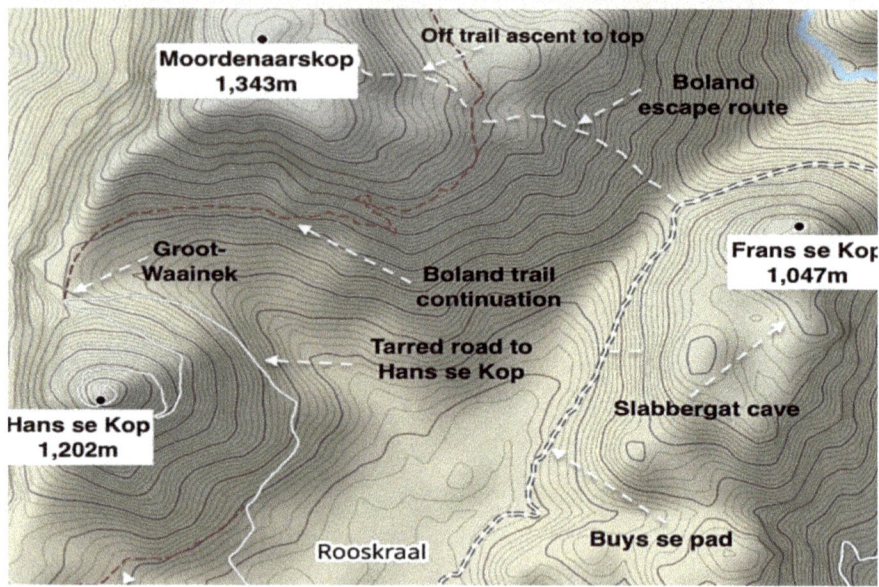

A dramatic name for a mountain, harbouring an even more dramatic history. Towards the end of the 18th century, it is said that travellers and isolated local farms were being robbed by a gang that had a hide out on or near the mountain. The then Cape Government decided that something had to be done to curb these bandits, so a commando group was organised, led by four field-cornets, and made up of burghers from Stellenbosch and Swellendam.

A search took place, and the robbers were finally located in a remote and difficult to reach ravine. A rope descent was needed, and Barend Saayman and one other volunteered to be lowered down to the hide out. In the resulting fire fight Saayman was killed by the brigands, whilst his fellow volunteer was badly injured. Further chase was abandoned but a short time later the robbers were caught, and those not shot were taken and hanged in Cape Town.

As recompense for the loss of Barend Saayman, the Directors of the Dutch East India Company directed that the Governor grant the widow of the man who had lost his life, a farm to be named Barend Saayman's Eredood – 'Barend Saayman's honourable death'. Each field-cornet was presented with an inscribed silver jug. The farm awarded to Barend Saayman's widow, situated in the Riversdale district, subsequently passed hands and became known as Surrey.

One of the inscribed silver jugs was known to still be in Stellenbosch, in the possession of a Mr Beyers. It would be wonderful if this item could be seen in a suitable museum.
Ref - Discovering Southern Africa. By T. V. Bulpin.

Moordenaarskop From the N2
Grade 4.5 B Orange 9 ½ hrs

At least this top is reachable from the N2 along the currently closed original Boland trail. Though it is a looooong day, at just short of 30km!

Take the old Boland trail from the view-point at the top of Sir Lowry's Pass and follow this until reaching the tarred road that leads up to Hans se Kop. The tarred road has nothing to recommend it, apart from the fact that it helps get you where you want to go. Once you reach Groot-Waainek, take a right to follow the old Boland trail once more, as it flanks the southern aspect of Moodenaarskop. Water is usually available from streams on this section.

At a point on the east side of the mountain, where the old escape route (recently re-cairned by friends and I), descends towards Buys se Pad, there is a large marker cairn. A short descent from the cairn takes you to a stream that issues forth from a kloof that ascends left up this side of Moordenaarskop. Take the ridge right of the stream – no trail – to climb up to the lowest of the mountain's three tops – point 1,334m.

You may be tired, but if you are anything like me, and considering that you would probably not be back this way again, I was determined to take in the highest point 1,343m that beckons some 200m away to the north. Oddly enough this highest point does not sport a concrete marker pillar and is only marked by a small pile of rocks. That distinction is given to the second highest top at 1,337m. This now lies 250m away south west across the stream watershed. Again – you may as well go there so as to take in all three tops. Besides the views are stupendous.

Slabbergat cave In a twist to the Moordenaarskop mystery. In January of 2020 Frans Slabber, an MCSA member, came across a rocky hole on the far side of an outlier mountain close to Moordenaarskop, A month later he returned, armed with some equipment and accompanied by Steve Chadwick and Clarissa Hughes they explored and found a cave system that penetrated right through the hillside to come out the other side. Too

The dramatic vista of Moordenaarskops west face after a heavy winter storm.

Looking south from the 1,337m top of Moordenaarskop towards Hans se Kop, Steenbras and Kogelberg.

small to have ever harboured shelter to humans. Nevertheless, deep into the cave they found two pieces of a very old ceramic jug. Maybe a robber or two hid here at one time?

As we pass southwest along the rim of the HH mountain range, the heights dramatically decrease. From Moordenaarskop at 1,340m the height drops down to 963m at Groot-Waainek. At this point the Boland trail leaves the tarred access road and heads off north to its isolation and beauty. After a final kick up to the 1,182m height of Hans se Kop, the continued hills never again climb up above 1,000m. The diminishing ridge then crosses the N2 highway and passes on in undulations before finally plunging into the sea at Steenbrasmond. But first, before we reach the sea, there is much of interest for the hardy hiker, scrambler and the just plain curious.

Hans se Kop, Sugar Loaf, Spitzkop, Verkykerskop – 1,182m
Grade 3B Orange Six hours.
There is one serious scrambling route on the west face (see rock climbing section, Page 130).

Take the route as for Moordenaarskop, but once gaining the tarmac communication towers service road, follow this by its tortious twists up to it summit.

Four names, one mountain. I stand to be corrected, but in the title above I have tried to place them in chronological order. Personally, I like Verkykerskop – Binocular top, so much more prosaic than Hans se

Magnificent West face of Hans se Kop.

Kop – 'The top belonging to Hans'........Though Spitzkop – Pointed Peak also has a nice ring to it, certainly descriptive of how the mountain looks.

Hans se Kop and on south

As the heights of Hans se Kop drops down, I have tried to piece together the routes created by these earlier pioneers, with those of our own modern-day travels. Without losing sight of what was probably travelled before by our forebears and more latterly the 'flower pickers', to whom we owe a great debt, and upon whose travels we owe many of today's hiking trails.

Our own scrambles are not claimed 1st ascents, but merely 'notes in time' of our own explorations.

As the south flank of Hans se Kop drops down, the first weaknesses appear in the lower cliffs to its right.

All 4's Gully. Grade 2.5C Orange.
17th Mar 2021. Chris Van Heever, Steve Chadwick, Clarissa Hughes.
Steep grass scrambling with exposure and fall potential towards the top. Unlikely to have been climbed before.

This line takes the first gully that appears as the flank of Hans se Kop drops down to the lower ridge. Follow the gully left until turning a cliff to find a steep grass groove which leads to an open finishing scoop. Useful rock holds on the left wall, before heading out right to climb the exposed steeper finishing rim. Descend by the Devils Craw or by walk out along the Boland (1 hr) to the old wagon trail.

Devils Craw. Grade 2.5B Orange.
27th Jul 2020. Steve Chadwick, Clarissa Hughes.

Grass and stream bed scrambling. This is the next gully right of All 4's Gully. Somewhat hidden from below, as it hides behind a buttress, but its left to right aspect becomes more open and obvious as you reach its base. Has been used as a descent from nearby harder ascents, bum sliding being a quick option on the steeper grass sections. Keep your legs together or the occasional rock could spoil your day. Alternatively, there is the 1 hour walk out along the Boland towards the old wagon trail.

Likely to have been climbed by Mr S. Rose and party pre 1932 – he writes: *'On Saturday…we… caught the 1.27 p.m. train from Town to Somerset West. At 3.15 p.m. we set off from the level crossing along the railway line, which we followed for some distance, before cutting off the last big loop, and striking up the slopes in the direction of the Spitzkop (Sugar Loaf). We crossed the line for the last time then we ascended the steep, grassy gully which runs up through the first few bands of rock on the west face, and on reaching the top climbed out to the right, and then up the broken rocks ahead. Judicious traversing backwards and forwards, including two long traverses to the left enabled us to break through the crags on this side of the peak, and landed us on top at 6.15 p.m.'*

It would seem the party used Devils Craw gully to reach the south face of Hans se Kop and then climbed the face by traversing between bands of rock.

I penned this verse marking our own ascent of the Devils Craw:

We set off in the dark of the night
Before the sky was cracked by the dawn
And parked in the shadow of the mountain
Just as the black gave way to the morn

The cold was bitter and chilling
We climbed as fast as breath would allow
Well wrapped in layers of clothing
Still no sweat would come to our brow

Slowly we toiled up the gully
The dark slit seemed to taunt us to try
It was as if it looked down to mock us
And I swear there was a glint in its eye

As we entered the base of the gully
We grasped anything to aid our ascent
Holding bushes and grass and hard rock
As our bodies contorted and bent

The dark came in all around us
As deeper inside we did tread
Into the maw of the mountain
With feelings of fear and of dread

Outside there was sun on the mountain
Inside there was loose rock and gloom
Holding rock that could fall on each other
That could spell our inevitable doom

But…slowly the angle eased back
As the throat it widened above
Perhaps, just perhaps we could do this
To survive and see the ones that we love

At the top the sunshine it warmed us
We built a cairn to mark where we had been
Would we ever come back to this gully?
Well maybe, all hikers they do like to dream

Now, as I sit on my stoep in the evening
And watch the sun set in crimson array
I sometimes look up at that mountain
To where the dragon allowed us to play

To the right of Dragons Craw there is a buttress seamed with possibilities. The following route takes a line on its right, and follows a steep right to left slanting weakness. A fortuitous liaison of an aging ex climber and a guy who can climb. This line is aesthetically pleasing as it cleaves its way in a straight line up towards an outcrop of rock that from below looks like a pimple, but is in fact a fine pinnacle.

Pimple Gully. Grade 2.5C Red.
18th Apr 2021. Raphael Shaw, Steve Chadwick. Steep grass scrambling leading to a chimney and a vertical grass and rock scrambling exit. Unlikely to have been climbed before.

Pimple Gully

SC Gully. Grade 2.5C Red.
8th Aug 2020. Helmut Schuster, Claudia Schuster, Nikola Schuster, Steve Chadwick.
For some distance to the right there is now an area of broken ground, leading into a steep gully with a slab of white rock at its base.

The original ascent by-passed the white slab by scrambling up a broken rake to the right, then crossed back left to climb two pitches to easier ground above. Nowhere difficult, but the first 150m has serious fall potential. Unlikely to have been climbed before.

The Ramp
Right of SC Gully is an area of broken ground that gradually lays back in angle to reach an area of steep grass we have provisionally called 'The Ramp'. Climbed by a Gantouw hike exploration party in 2018, the 'Ramp' is also crossed from low right to upper left by a now very faint 'flower pickers' trail.

Exiting the rock groove on the 3rd pitch of SC Gully.

The Ramp and Klipspringer Gully.

Difficult to say for certain, but we think this is the way H. B. Begley and party ascended pre 1917, when he writes: *'There is no difficulty about obtaining the permission of the occupiers of Applegarth (as Goedeverwachting was known then) to pass through the farm... and having crossed the line, one follows the path that wends its way up the slopes on the opposite side of the loop or "hair pin" bend formed by the railway. After re-crossing the rails, the path continues up the mountain slope in the north-easterly direction, passes over the crest of the ridge.'*

Flower pickers from Cape Town Aldderley Street flower market came this way, and to this day Rasta folk still climb the lower slopes in search of Buchu and the many other herbs that are used for medicinal purposes. The well-known botanist and collector T. P. Stokoe also came this way on more than one occasion, often guided by flower pickers.

In the excellent book 'T. P. Stokoe the man, the myths, the flowers' by Peter Slingsby and Amida Johns, we read: *'The spring of 1954 found TP in the Hottentot Holland Mountains, in the Rooskraal valley behind Verkykerskop – the pyramid shaped peak above Sir Lowry's Pass...TP's flower pickers were nearby'*

Gazing up to the Nek of 'Klipspringer Gully.

66

Klipspringer Gully 2B Orange.
24th Feb 2021. Clarissa Hughes, Steve Chadwick.

Another exercise in Covid frustration. Likely to have been climbed before, as it is an obvious line of weakness. Approach by using the Hepic trail until its high point sees you below and left of the gully. Taking the diagonal line up to the gully and ascending the left-hand fork presents no difficulties other than the usual rough and often loose terrain. There really was a Klipspringer bouncing around as we approached the gulley proper.

There follows another rise up to 625m then a dip to a Nek straddled by what we have called the Sugar Cube.

Troll left hand 2B Orange
23rd Mar 2021. Clarissa Hughes, Patsy Mockford Steve Chadwick.

Exiting the rock groove on the 3rd pitch of SC Gully.

Another line likely taken by H. V. Begley and party who also wrote in 1917 *"…it serves as a quick and pleasant way of getting from Sir Lowry's Pass into the upper Steenbrass valley…..This path strikes away from the pass road some few miles away from the (SLP) village, crossing the railway line at the gates ahead, then makes for a gully in the north-easterly direction, via the Nek of which it arrives in the Steenbrass valley.'*
As we approached the Nek left of the cube on our own ascent we came across a very old rusty opened tin of sardines. Could the tin be carbon dated to 1917?

Troll Gully (right hand) 2B Orange
17th Feb 2021 Clarissa Hughes, Frans Slabber, Steve Chadwick.
Takes the rake to the top of the right-hand gully. Again, almost certainly ascended before,

Frans Slabber (alias the Troll) and Steve Chadwick approaching the top of troll gully right hand.

though there is no sign of a flower pickers trail.
The Gully of the Troll - Waxing lyrical again
*Now the Princess, the Troll and the Wizard
Set off in the grey early light
Not sure yet as to where they would wander
But they would climb wherever they might*

*The track led them on ever upwards
As they shared stories and had some good crack
Whilst above them the wind of the mountain
Whispered "maybe you'd better turn back"*

*Onwards and upwards they hiked
Though the sun had yet to show forth
Where would they go up the mountain?
But a weakness would show in due course*

*Now the Troll was on an agenda
To clear alien trees from the land
He drew cutlass from inside his rucksack
And swung with his massive right hand.*

With alien fir trees destroyed
As he hacked this way and that
Sweat beaded on the Trolls massive brow
And he lost a few kilos of fat

Above them a square plug of rock
Stood sheer with power imbued
So, in a moment of sheer idiocy
They called it the Great Sugar Cube

Direct was out of the question
But to go leftwards, upwards, or right?
So the Princess led us up rightwards
Into brightness and away from the night

From the shadow they climbed into sunshine
And the gully was left to its shade
They laid a cairn to show where they'd crested
So others might see what they'd made

Humility humbled the three
As they thanked gods that their climb was stress free
But there was a glint in the eye of the Troll
For he'd seen another alien tree

The ridge from Hans se Kop to Gantouw (Eland Pass)

During the past few years we explored the entire ridge in detail between Hans se Kop and the N2, this was with a certain amount of madness and determination, as in most places the Boland Trail is only a short distance below. The undulating ridge direct provides some interesting scrambling with many 'hands on' sections and occasional more serious down climbing.

At the Nek down from point 631 and just prior to reaching the Gantouw itself we came across a curious raised platform. It must have taken two to three strong guys to lift the sometime large rocks so as to erect a large platform. Not to dwell inside, as the space inside was also deliberately filled in, but perhaps to provide a plinth a 'viewing' type platform? Experts in the field have been consulted, and we are advised that the native Khoekhoe people were not in the habit of constructing stone structures. We are left with conjecture as to why early European peoples would have made such a structure.

There were brigands who operated from dens on the far side of Moordenaarskop, also there were robbers who operated out of the Hangklip area and lived in caves there-about. Perhaps

Where the 'Upper Trail' breaches the rim. Some 200 m left of the 'Wagon Trail' the wall structure may be seen centre left.

A closer view.

this was a lookout point used by robbers, who could from this vantage point espy travellers and pick out solitary wagons to rob.

Rita Blake in her excellent 'History of Rooiels' writes: *'The Hangklip area was a refuge for runaway slaves, Strandlopers, deserters and sailors jumping ship. This band was relatively successful as there were plenty of fish, veldkos and game, even buffalo and eland, and they had weapons and their own boat. How-ever they also wanted sheep, cattle and luxuries, and raided farms near Somerset West and Kleinmond for these. They ambushed and robbed wagons bringing produce to the Cape market over the Elandspad (the old pass near Sir Lowry's Pass).'*

Interestingly, in the context of possible bandits operating at Gantouw (Elandspad), we once more come across the name Barend Simon in a story too close in details to be disentangled from the Moordenaarskop tale. Over time stories become blurred and legends even merge. The only hard thread seems to be that Barend Simon / Saayaman did exist and was a hero.

Rita Blake again " *At the end of the 18th century, these bands raided a party crossing the pass, killed the servants and took the cattle and two children …. to the cave in the Rooiels Kloof. They wanted someone literate to forge pass documents for them and the girl was forced to do so. She included a sentence saying that they had been captured and were being held in a cave along the coast. The veldkornet, Jan Linde, let some cattle graze near the Steenbras River and watched them from hiding. When the drosters came to steal them he followed the party, but they moved to the cave at Pringle Bay and barricaded the mouth holding the children there as hostages. At length, Barend Simon let himself down with a rope to the entrance, shot the leader and rescued the children. About 40 drosters were shot - only one old woman is said to have survived.'*

History of Gantouw – (Eland Path) & the New Sir Lowry's Pass

In the decades, even centuries before the wagon trail was used, it is thought that there were earlier paths through this area of the Hottentot Holland mountain rim. Evidence of this may be found in a curious small wall, with its centre contemporaneously filled in. The purpose of this structure is not known, but it lies some 200m north east and up slope from the top of the wagon trail summit, and marks the high point of a faint trail that ascends up from the left – above the wagon trail. Thus it may have been the original way the rim was breached, perhaps being used by the Khoekhoe people.

An imaginative 1796 engraving of 'Hottentot Holland Kloffie'

Post fires, when the ground is clear, another lower trail may be seen rising more directly up the kloof right of the wagon trail. Henry Lichtenstein in 1806 writes *'the course of this road has changed many times, and the old cattle trail is now overgrown and disused for some 30 years.'*

It seems likely this reference is to the old cattle trail that took the kloof more directly, and that the wagon trail we know today was developed for the exact purpose of moving wagons over the pass, as both the upper left and right hand (kloof) trails are too steep for wagons.

The Old Pass

Long before man ever travelled up the pass, herds of eland, searching for greener pastures, crossed in this area in the winter months. Traditionally migratory elephants led by the herd's matriarch, would make their way down to their grazing grounds on the Cape Flats. A

Khoekhoe tribe, known as Gantauwers (People of the Eland) also followed this pass. They called the path T'kanna Ouwe or Gantouw, 'Gan / ikhan' being the Khoekhoe word for eland and 'touw' the Khoekhoe word for path or pass. Later travellers also took up this meaning, calling it the Elandspad (path of the eland). Later still - ox wagon travellers called it the 'Hottentots Holland Kloof.

It was early cattle buyers like Hendrik Lacus and Jeronimus Cruse, sent in 1663 by Zacharias Wagenaar - the replacement for Jan van Riebeeck as Commander at the Cape - who were possibly the first Europeans to brave the path over the nek.

It is believed that in 1689 'Isaac Schrijver' took the first wagon – unloaded – over the pass. The goods being carried up by slaves.

From Cape Town to the Pass

It is worth noting, although often overlooked, that the Gantouw was not the only obstacle that had to be overcome in order to leave Cape Town and head east. The 'Cape Flats' was a notorious place for the bogging down of wagons in thick sand. As a consequence there was no 'one road' across the Flats, as wagon drovers tried not to follow the tracks of a previous vehicle that had broken through the thin top stable layer of sand.

Even on the lower hills, passing the present Sir Lowry's Pass village, wagons had to overcome the 'Roode Hoogte' or the 'Red Heights', another area of unstable ground through which the wagoneers tried to pick an independent way. This is well illustrated in the water colour below of the Hottentots Holland mountain pass, with its myriad of tracks in the foreground. The actual line of the pass beyond is also quite accurately depicted as it snakes its way up and round the mountainside.

On the right a photo taken in March 2021 from approximately the same position as the water colour left. Showing the Toll House as it is now with the grooves of the wagon trails still visible above curving up the 'Roode Hoogte' hill behind the 'Tolhuys'.

Explorer, Author and Artist (John) Thomas Baines writes. *"After an early breakfast, we mounted our horses, and almost immediately commenced the ascent which leads to the pass called Hottentot-Holland Kloof. At the first part of it, the road is not very steep, but as soon as the traveller enters the hollow way of the Roode Hoogte (the Red Heights) the difficulty of the ascent begins. This is a lower hill forming the foot of the*

mountain, and composed of a hard, barren, reddish, clayey, ferruginous earth, into which the road, towards its summit, is cut down to the depth of, perhaps, twenty feet. After this he has to climb the rocky mountain itself, and will not, without some surprise, behold loaded waggons ascending and descending so steep and frightful a road……The danger in which both oxen and waggon are placed while passing the mountains, renders the utmost care and vigilance indispensable. For should they become restive, and deviate from the proper road, or obstinately refuse to draw, the waggon would be thrown down the precipice, dragging them, and perhaps the driver also, along with it to inevitable destruction."

On the right a photo taken in March 2021 from approximately the same position as the 1786 water colour by Jan Brandes. Showing the Toll House as it is now with the grooves of the wagon trails still visible above curving up the 'Roode Hoogte' hill behind the 'Tolhuys'.

In 1808 - 97 ox wagons were recorded to have used the pass. In 1820, this number had increased to 2,800; which indicates perhaps 7 to 8 a day, given good weather. As the upper pass is definitely one way only, a system of early traffic control was introduced.

Extra oxen being hired for the ascent from farms near the base of the pass such as Goedeverwachting (built in 1795) with each wagon using up to 24 span oxen for the ascent. The nearby 'Cloevermaaker's Huys' was used as a Toll House, each loaded wagon being charged four shillings. These early travellers were extremely challenged by the steep and rocky ascent. Oxen were frequently killed and wagons smashed as they lost ground and fell back down the mountain. The route was so severe that more than a fifth of the wagons were damaged. Thus it became expedient at times to unload the wagons, take them up piece by piece, and reassemble them at the summit, while the oxen and travellers scrambled up over the rocks. Grooves in the rocks made by the brake drag-shoes which locked the wheels on the descent on the wagons can still be seen in the rock of the pass after 250 years.

During the early 1800's a small maintenance gang was employed to keep the pass in reasonable shape. If you look carefully you may see that stones have been shaped and let into the deeper old grooves of the pass. The capping maintenance stones themselves have then been worn down with their own grooves. Sad to say that off road bikers sometimes illegally use the pass, and as they accelerate they often 'kick' out these maintenance capping stones.

In one place an embankment was constructed to widen the track, as well as a stone walled pen to house animals whilst the wagons were being hauled up the pass.

Improvements were gradually made, but it was never other than a hazardous undertaking. The missionary Latrobe wrote in 1816 *"I found the accounts of the formidable passage by no means exaggerated. Twenty-four oxen having been sent out from Genadendal to meet us, our complement had increased to 54 and it was with difficulty that even this number drew the loaded wagons up the rugged road."*

In 1797 Lady Anne Barnard, who made the trip up the kloof declared, *"The path to the top was very perpendicular and the jutting rocks over which the wagon was to be pulled were so large that we were astonished how it was accomplished at all. Particularly at one point called -The Porch".*

Towards the end of the 18th century the pass was once used by a certain married man who ran away with a beautiful slave girl called Zara. His wife sued for divorce and also that his name should be struck off any records.

The below drawing by William Burchell depicts wagon teams that have crested the top of the Hottentots Holland Kloof. The scene as they continue their trek east seems almost tranquil with relief, as they leave the struggle of the kloof ascent behind them.

The next photo was taken in May 2021, whilst trying to stand where William Burchell stood whilst make his painting some 270 years ago.

The Gantouw Pass cannons

A short path up from the crest takes you to the signal cannons. In 1734 the VOC – Dutch East India Company. Introduced the 'Dutch Call-Up Cannon signal system', which eventually consisted of 54 strategically placed cannons. The system was designed to help Burghers form a communication link between Cape Town fort and the outlying districts, and was designed to be effective as far as Citrusdal in the North, Worcester to the North east, and Swellendam to the South East. Each cannon had a dedicated gunner who lived nearby and who was responsible for firing the next cannon in the chain.

A threat to Cape Town activated the signal system and Burghers from far flung districts would hurry to its defence.

In answer to the cannons, in July 1795, one hundred and sixty-eight mounted men from Swellendam under the command of Jacobus Delport, answered the call and rode down through the kloof. The Dutch troops under Colonel Robert Jacob Gordon surrendered to the British on the 16th September. This was the first of two British take overs of the Cape Colony.

The signal system was used for the 5th and last time in January 1806, when the British landed at Blaauwberg. Thereafter the cannon signal system was abandoned.

It is understood that the Helderberg Renaissance Foundation is trying to restore the cannons to firing condition, and also to conduct this event on National Heritage Day 24th September each year.

The pass was declared a national monument in 1958.
Two views of the old Toll House, originally called 'Cloevermaaker Huys'. The left photo being taken after the building was no longer in use as a 'Toll House', i.e. post the opening of the new 1830 pass. The building then being allowed to fall into disrepair.

In the photo on the right - taken March 2021 from almost the same vantage point - we may still see similar trees and the same mountain skyline. In the late 1800's the structure was rehabilitated and was in use as a dwelling until the late 1990's.

A stop before reaching the 'Toll Huis' may well have been at 'Brinks Inn', now known as Goedeverwachting. The original buildings of 'The Inn' stand near the road some 100m up from the current larger house, and are still used as dwellings.

In a more recent twist of history, politicians of that time needed a secluded base near Cape Town, where they might discuss issues regarding the imminent release of Nelson Mandela from prison on Robben island. The Old Toll House was chosen as an ideal secluded location where plans and decisions could be made, away from media attention. Nelson Mandela was released on February 11, 1990.

The building now has been allowed to fall back into ruin.

The New Pass
It was Lt-General Sir Gailbraith Lowry Cole, Governor of the Cape Colony from 1828 to 1833, who instigated improvements to this pass.

He requested that Major C. C. Mitchell inspect the Kloof pass with a view to making improvements. This done, Major Mitchell drew up a plan showing that a new road with easy gradients could be built south of the old kloof. The estimated cost being £7,000.

Work was authorised by Sir Lowry in 1829, without the Secretary of State's permission, whereupon Sir Lowry was ticked off: "Build at your expense!" However, the UK government later relented and agreed to pay for the new pass.

The new road, which finally cost £7,011, was completed using convict labour and was opened on 6 July 1830. Initially there was a toll gate at the top of the pass.
The original Toll Keepers house at the summit of Sir Lowry's Pass. An 1832 pen and wash drawing by Charles D'Oyly. Note the accurate portrayal of the hills of West Peak and the Dome in the background.

The above photo was taken in May 2021. Difficult now to stand where Charles D'Oyly sat some 189 years ago, as blasting for the new road had completely obliterated his view point. However the view point on the left (on the right of the current viewing car park) does contain elements of the stone foundation of the original Toll keeper's house.

The rock outcrop in Charles D'Oyly's drawing is an exact portrayal of the rock outcrop shown in the 2021 photo.

Right again – the parapet wall still stands just before the old road passes the outcrop and reaches the Toll Keeper's house. Whilst the sweep of the new road looks almost in place for the 1832 drawing. The road remained narrow to the extent that vehicles could pass each other only at selected points on the route. In the 1930s, the pass was widened and tarred; it was further improved in 1956 when it was further widened.

Photos of the new road in 1895.

In 1984 the upper parts were widened to four lanes through a reinforced concrete construction at a cost of R4.5 million.

Two historical uses of the new pass

November 1832.
Lt Duthie was courting the daughter of George Rex (reported to be an illegitimate son of Prince George – afterward George III) in Knysna. Because he was enjoying his courtship and was very much in love he left his departure to the last minute. It took him five days to gallop madly through torrential rain, swim rivers, change horses, descend the pass and race through Somerset West at sundown, to reach the castle at 11 o'clock, with one hour to spare to the expiry of his leave.

December 1835
In retaliation for incessant cattle raids on the eastern frontier, on 11 December 1834 a Cape government commando killed a Xhosa chief of high rank, thus incensing the tribesmen. An army of 10,000 men, led by Maqoma, a brother of the slain chief, swept across the frontier into the Colony, pillaging and burning homesteads and killing all who resisted. Survivors

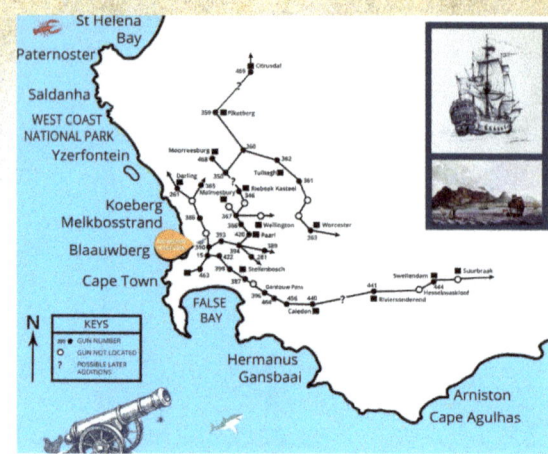

A young C. C. Michell   *Sites of the VOC 'Call Up' gun signal system*

sheltered in Grahamstown. Lt-Colonel Harry Smith was sent to relieve the settlers and made the 600 miles to Grahamstown on 6 January 1835, just six days after leaving Cape Town.

Compiled with grateful thanks from the following References:
Peggy Heap – The story of Hottentots Holland.
Dr Ivor Jardine. Personal communication & 1957 MCSA journal – Hottentots Holland Kloof.
Dr Janette Deacon - Personal communication
Henry Lichtenstein – Travels in Southern Africa 1803 - 1806
WWW.Nitidacannonstation.co.za
Ryan Norris, Lesley Cirillo, David Byers – SLP residents.
Wikipedia.com
Mari Fouché - The story of Sir Lowry's Pass

1956 the Summit' cafe at the current view point car park. Copyright unknown

'Summit' cafe with post 1950's road.

A shard of pottery on the Elands Pass

I led a hike party up the Elands pass today, and as we toiled up the steepest section near the summit, a group member spotted a shard of pottery.

How many wagons had faltered here and had fallen back down the steep rocks. How many oxen had died in an agony of broken bones?

215 years later, a sharp-eyed hiker caught sight of something on the side of the pass. It was a piece of old Dutch pottery which has been reasonably dated to late 1700's early 1800's.

Sometimes I see something that immediately sends my mind into a kaleidoscope of often conflicting thoughts. A mixture of 'what if', 'how' and 'what led to this shard to be where it was', and 'when'.

Here is the story that my mind saw:
The Dutch family had moved out from Holland, hoping to start a new life in what was then, almost the ends of the earth. It may as well have been, as they knew they would never see Amsterdam again.

Life had been tough working on a homestead near Cape Town, but slowly they had accumulated enough money to afford to begin the trek away from British rule, and its lack of respect for their Dutch language and way of life.

They planned long, and finally committed to join a small group of trekkers heading East to a land they could call their own and to live a lifestyle not dictated by a foreign power.

For two days the party had toiled through the sand flats that separated Cape Town from the arable land of Somerset West.

Finally, they had halted for the night at the bottom of the feared Elands pass, and as the sun had set that night, they had gazed up at the mountain side as it turned to crimson, then black to match the night sky as the sun plunged into the sea to the west beyond Cape Town. They wondered how it could be ascended by man, let alone by an ox wagon that contained all their treasured possessions. With that thought they drifted off into a fitful sleep.

The morning had been born into a blue sky, with a promise of fortune over the hill. The group had negotiated for the use of an extra sixteen oxen to be able to pull their wagons up the pass. Guides had been hired that knew every rock on the ascent. But nothing guaranteed success.

The way had begun easily enough, but as they slowly gained height the way became precipitous. They passed deep grooves in the rock carved out by the locked iron clad wheels of those wagons coming down the pass.

Approaching the summit, they might have been forgiven for thinking 'we have made it.' But that would have been too soon for the last drag was the most frightening section of all.
Ropes were run through eyelets fixed into the last rocks to give extra stability. These were connected to the front of each wagon. Whips were cracked. The oxen pulled almost with a willingness, for they knew from the past that their efforts would soon be over when they reached the top.

Ships were seen from Signal hill above Cape Town. The signal cannon was fired, and it was answered by a second cannon between Cape Town and Somerset West. This was the pre-arranged signal that ships were coming in, and that farmers on the other side of the Hottentot Holland mountain range should bring their produce to Cape Town The signal cannon at the top of the pass also fired its shot to the east.

The cannon fire startled the animals and the more skittish of them let out a bellow and lunged forward.

Their wagon jumped a rut and teetered. Almost in slow motion the wagon fell sideways, dragging the oxen with it. Down it crashed, a tangle of wagon, belongings and animals. The driver cursed but could do nothing except jump out of the way to save his own life.

The dust settled but it left their belongings scattered across the hillside, along with a broken wagon and mutilated oxen with compound fractured bones glinting with blood as the

shattered bone ends protruded through the skin.

The driver had seen it before, but that didn't make it any easier.

He took his gun and put a bullet through the head of each bellowing animal and the mountainside echoed to the shots. Then, finally there was silence.

Contemporary painting of a wagon ascending a pass. Note the men on the hillside with ropes

South African wagons and their oxen

The wagons of North America, Australia and South Africa all served a similar purpose at a similar time, each one reflecting the required attributes, artisan skills, knowledge and to some extent - the wood available at the time of construction. Even the South African wagon morphed along different lines depending on material available and requirements. This article dwells on the typical wagon of burden used to transport produce to and from Cape Town and the Boer Trekkers heading north and east.

The English word 'wagon or waggon' derives from the Dutch 'waghen' which is similar to the Old English word 'waegn' or wain, and thus is how the word 'wainwright – wagon builder – comes about.

Wagon Construction

The South African wagon is a different vehicle from that of the contemporaneous American West 'Prairie Schooner', being more closely related to the old European 'waggons'. It was realised early on that due to the terrain of many high passes and river crossings, the South African wagon needed to be able to be dismantled and hauled up and down steep rocky passes and across rivers, then to be reassembled once the obstacle was overcome.

They also needed to be able to flex without tearing themselves apart, thus tightly bolted sections were minimised in favour of flexible joints and wooden pins.

Above is a watercolour painting by the English Artist, Surveyor and Traveller Charles Mitchell of oxen pulling a wagon up the old Cradock Pass, Outeniqua Mountains, 1840. In this image, Michell records a Cape-wagon without rising wainscoting.

A typical wainscoting curved 'jawbone' rear of the wagon. An ox-wagon traditionally made with the sides rising toward the rear of the wagon to resemble the lower jawbone of an animal, was also known as a 'kakebeenwa' (jaw-bone wagon) Note the hanging chain and brake shoes.

In this drawing of William Burchell's wagon on the right, the brake shoes are in position under the wheel. They are held in place by the chains, one to a wheel spoke, which would lock the wheel, and one to the 'skid' upon which the wheel would slide on the descent. Which is, of course, how the well-known grooves we see today in the pass, were formed.

Quoting from Lucille Davie's article 'Step into a wagon and go back 200 years' - Eric Holm notes that 17 varieties of wood were used in wagon making. 'We have 800 woods here, whereas in Europe there's not much selection. South African woods were the best in the world for wagon making.'

It was imperative that the wagon shaft be manufactured from a very strong wood, usually stinkwood (Prunus Africana) or Ironwood (Olea capensis). In early days at the Cape, stinkwood was the most favoured wood for all wagon components. However as this wood was favoured by Cabinetmakers too, these trees were rapidly cut own and were replaced by ironwood.

The available types of wood ranged from the hardy yellowwood, abundant in the Cape at the time, to the boekenhout, a softish wood which would act as a kind of shock absorber but at the same time would stay firmly in position.

The bed-boards were built from Outeniqua yellowwood (podocarpus falcatus) and were approximately 4 centimetres thick.

These side-planks were generally made from yellowwood and the rungs (leerskeie) were made of Assegai wood (Curtisia dentate)

'The wheels were made of three or four kinds of wood... the nave yellowwood; wheel spokes were made of assegai wood at the Cape for its superb compressive and elastic-strength, as well as its fine grain. An additional quality is its low-shrinkage – a vital quality for tight-fitted spokes.

For the felloe – (the wooden rim upon which the iron rim is heat shrunk onto) red alder or white pear. The tyre was put on in one piece when hot, so as to draw and bind the whole of the wheel firmly together'.

The 'disselboom' connects the rear and strongest oxen to the front wheels of the wagon and was found to be the most effective way to yoke a team of oxen to a wagon so that they could pull efficiently.

On a descent, if the wagon started to roll more quickly than the oxen were walking, the relative forward movement of the shaft (disselboom) would take up the short slack of the rear-oxen's yoke rope and push it forwards against the oxen's horns, signalling to the rear-oxen to bare-backwards and thus slow down the wagon.

This is the reason why oxen had to maintain a fine set of bracing horns. If one of these rear-oxen died, a replacement ox from the rest of the span had to have horns. Thus, no trek oxen were ever shorn of their prongs. It was imperative that the strongest, stoutest and most experienced oxen be in-spanned into this position.

The Skidpan/brake-shoe 'Remskoen'

On a steep descent, if braking failed, and a wagoneer was unable to apply a shoe-brake to the wheels, then a runaway wagon would run-over and crush the oxen or pull them to their deaths. Thus, in the event that the oxen themselves could not slow the descent of a wagon; an efficient method of braking was essential.

Early Cape-wagons did not have the screw-applied braking of later transport wagons – shown on the right.

What they did have were 'skidpans' or remskoene (brake-shoes). Attached to the front of the wagon just aft of the front carriage were two lengths of iron chain having at their ends a wooden or iron shoe about 45 by 60 centimetres in length and shaped something like an open Dutch clog. The chain was only long enough to allow the shoe to slip under the rear wheel so that the wheel's rim fitted snugly into a groove in the shoe. In a sense the brake shoes acted as miniature sleds, thus slowing the speed of the wagon.

Protea nitida (Wagontree or 'Waboom')
The name 'waboom' was first recorded in 1720 and has thus been used for far longer than its scientific name.

There is a tradition that the name 'waboom' originates from the use of the wood for wheel rims and brake blocks for the wagons. Though Waboom wood was sometimes used - as noted above rooiels (Red Alder) or white pear were preferred for the 'felloe' or rim wood.
It seems that the preferred material for sledge' brake shoes was iron. It is doubtful that even waboom wood would be strong enough for this purpose. In later wagons, when 'screw applied braking was introduced, it could have been that waboom wood was used as the preferred brake pad material.

To this day, waboom proteas are abundant on the Hottentots Holland wagon pass. The bark sometimes bears witness to being used as the scratch pads by leopards, their scratch marks being visible somewhat disconcertingly high up the protea trunk.

However, the use of the waboom in wagons appears to have stopped early on, and surviving wagons built in 1795 and 1860 contain no wagon tree wood. Some firewood cutters maintain that the name comes from the use of wagon trees as sleds for hauling firewood down the mountains.

The oxen
The wagons themselves were some 5.5 metres long and 1.8 metres wide.

A painting of Cape Dutch farmers trekking by artist I. R. Skelton. Shows quite well how the oxen were harnessed.

A painting of Cape Dutch farmers trekking by artist I. R. Skelton. Again, shows how the oxen were harnessed. A riverbank at the site of a drift (crossing point) could become a quagmire due to the churning hooves of oxen and the deep rutting of wheels. It was common to have to wait days or even weeks for a drift to dry out for it to be possible to cross.

The great rear wheels were shod with a centimetre of iron and could stand nearly 2metres high. The smaller front wheels turned on a pivoted axle. The oxen were yoked two by two, each in its assigned place, with – as noted – the strongest pair on the disselboom. The most experienced pair were in the lead. The driver carried a long whip, and rode or walked alongside the beasts, with the 'Voorlooper' walking in front.

Over the years two breeds of oxen had been developed. Short compact beasts of great endurance, and a tall breed of enormous strength for sandy country and steep mountain tracks. The teams were often matched in colour, the Boers preferring mixed red and white animals; they had an aversion to plain white or grey oxen. Every adult farmer wished to own such a span, and was not considered successful until he did so.

Oxen required eight hours a day to graze, a further eight hours to rest while their grazed fodder passed through their multiple stomachs and was regurgitated as cud to be chewed again. This left eight hours a day for work.

If oxen were driven eight hours or more in a day with heavy loads followed by poor grazing, they would begin to die. It was essential that the oxen were outspanned (unyoked) for at least 16 hours a day. If they were driven through rain, and not dried, the hide on their shoulders would not only chafe at the harnesses, but would peel off in strips. Care of the beasts was paramount as flies would swarm on any wound.

If a team was kept in harness for the full eight hours, they would then need several days to recover. It was usual for a team to be outspanned around midday for about two hours. In this way, under ideal conditions, a team of oxen might move its wagon 20 kilometres in a day. A mountain pass or river crossing drift or donga (ravine) could take several days, since the load might have to be unloaded and carried by hand, whilst the wagon was dismantled, carried across the obstacle, then reassembled and the oxen re-spanned.

A sketch by Alice Balfour showing the 'voorlooper' (leader) leading the oxen across a river

Grateful thanks to References:
'Protea Atlas'
Sanbi PlantZA
Graham Leslie McCallum – 'The Cape wagon, a pictorial trek'
The Heritage Portal - Lucille Davie
https://www.lucilledavie.co.za/post/2009/10/30/step-into-a-wagon-and-go-back-200-years
Donald R. Morris – The washing of the spears.
Wikipedia
W. Burchell – Travels in the Interior of Southern Africa

N2 to the sea

Gordon's Bay, the Spine Ridge, Steenbras Dams. A fine pic courtesy of Jean Tresfon

As we cross the N2 the high mountains are left behind us; but 'It's not over until the fat lady sings'.

It's been a great journey that started with West Peak, and now there is but a little way to go.

Steenbras dams:
Work began on the lower dam in 1918 and was completed three years later. Additional height was added to the dam wall in 1928. The Upper Steenbras Dam was completed in 1977.

The access road from Clarence Drive built to service the filtration plant, was built in the 1940's, and is one of the only roads in South Africa with a hairpin bend greater than 180 degrees.

Sometimes when I am on a late night / early morning Farm Watch patrol, the lights of the high filtration plant seem to hang like a flying saucer above Gordons Bay.

Interesting to note that during the small hours of the morning, when the electricity demand is low, the Steenbras turbine power is used to pump water from the lower Steenbras to the upper. Such that water is then available to run downhill from the upper to the lower Steenbras to drive the turbines so that power is available for your morning cup of coffee.

Ridge access

This final section of the Rim's march to the sea is known by some as 'Dinosaur Ridge'. Looking at its spiny back we might more accurately call it 'Stegosaurus Ridge'.

If entry was allowed it would be possible to hike to the ridge from almost anywhere on the Gordon's Bay side. But be aware that the water authorities do not allow access, and they are zealous guardians.

'Danie Miller' trail is the only trail on the Gordon's Bay side of the ridge, and as such has long been used by local residents and hikers as a local fitness tester. There have been security issues, so it is best to hike the trail in groups.

The Danie Miller trail Grade 1.5A Orange. 7.5Km Time 4hrs.
Rocky for much of the way, especially when just past the GB hillside sign.

A co-hiker Wim Van Nunen at the Danie Miller trail start

This is a mountainside / coast circuit combining the Danie Miller trail with a pleasant return along the coast. This is certainly as low as this guide gets.

Begin on the beach car park of Gordon's Bay and set off up the road towards the main Gordon's Bay road. Cross the junction heading for the right-hand side of the Sir Lowry's Pass Rd, and after 20m turn right and follow Grens Rd as it climbs up the hill past four right hand turn off's until you are able to turn right at Chapman Ave. Shortly you will be able to turn left up Aurora Drive, and almost immediately you will find yourself on a corner which is the start of the Danie Miller trail proper.

Step steeply up the concrete drive for 20m until you can turn right onto the sign posted trail. The way gradually contours up above the tree line to take in great views across False Bay to the far away hills of Table Mountain and Silvermine. A stunning vantage point at sunset.

The path remains reasonable going as it crosses two streams that will be flowing during winter, until you reach the bottom of the huge GB sign that spreads its white way up the hillside above you.

Students from the Naval training base below you are

Beautiful views from the Danie Miller trail
West Peak to Hans se Kop
The Strand & Gordon's Bay

occasionally tasked with running directly up to the GB sign as part of their physical training. Sometimes carrying tins of white paint to 'brush up' the GB sign itself.

The rough path now steps diagonally down over a few rocky steps where it is possible to lose your way. But have faith as the path does carry on until it reaches the fire break that runs down from the water works above.

It is now possible to go down slope to the road. Swing left then down back right to enter Waboom road. Turn left for a few meters to find a path down to Clarence Drive.

Now cross Clarence and follow it right and on down to the Bikini Beach turn off. Pass by the Thirsty Oyster watering hole; unless you are feeling thirsty after your hike, in which case drop by for a drink. Then follow Beach Road and seaside paths back to your car.

Caves of the ridge:

Research and exploring this ridge over a number of years has revealed unexpected hidden places. With knowledge comes responsibility, such that as a result of discussions with friends of the great outdoors, I have reluctantly decided that though I write up the story of these caves, I may not describe how to reach them. I realise this is counter intuitive, and my defence for this is on sticky ground, but we feel to reveal the location of these caves would lead to them being trashed, used as toilets, and generally abused. Such is a reflection on our society. Be aware that the hike to these caves is via steep unstable ground. You should be an experienced hiker and wear strong hiking footwear. If you do find your way to any of these caves, please respect their history, and do not litter or otherwise spoil these special places.

Owl Crag Cave

High on the left on the Gordons Bay side of the ridge lies Owl crag and cave. The cave walls unfortunately already spoilt by graffiti. Friends of mine visiting recently have removed litter and broken glass. If you do find this secluded place, please do not visit during nesting season. This retreat would comfortably sleep 4-5.

Owl Crag Cave

Leg rings of doomed pigeons taken in flight by resident Owls.

'De Landrost Hof' Cave

Wherever possible I like to use original narrative, so what follows is the story as related to me by Andy Connell:

'We discovered the "De Landrost Hof" late one afternoon.......the cavern has been used as a refuge twice in recent history. The first dweller to occupy the cave is still there.

Andy Connell and family inside De Landrost Hof' cave. Circa 2001.

A body lies interred covered in rocks, just inside the entrance, and a small diary we found by his cross tells us the story. A certain Herr Rudy Kleber was a German emigrant, who suddenly found his status as a lawyer in Cape Town, was changed to 'Alien', by the British government at the outbreak of WWII in September 1939.

His future was to be interned on either Robben Island or another

'Camp' as an alien for the duration of the war.....He managed to escape arrest by fleeing Cape Town....so he became a fugitive in his new homeland.

Just how Herr Kleber managed to find this cavern is not told, but the ex-Landrost of Cape Town lived there until he became ill and was buried on his death by a person he mentions only as 'Kapi'.

Kapi must have lived locally and helped him with provisions from the town. Apparently Herr Rudy also trapped food, so may have had some small reserves. His diary, in old style German tells of his flight, his finding of Kapi, and his weakening state over the winter of 1940. It ends with his feverish complaint of cold, hunger and of the pain of being so alone.

Kapi returned one day to find Herr Rudy dead. He laid the body within the entrance of the cavern, covering the lifeless form with a pile of stones and erecting a cross. His ghost remains inside the cave, protecting the sanctity of its own grave. Sometimes at night you may hear the rustle of disturbed stones on the scree slopes outside, or the moan of his desolate loneliness.

Exploring the back passages of De Landrost Hof.

Even today, spending a night in the cave, sleeping next to the burial mound of stones, remains a serious mental challenge.

The cave must have been found by a second dweller who occupied the cavern briefly for a few days, or occasionally for short times only. He must have been superstitious to have left the grave and its diary alone. The bottles and enamel dishes found all suggest a time of around the late seventies. Other broken beer and Fanta bottles found at the cave were all removed.'

Thus far I hope that the reader has been drawn along by the pathos of this sad and fascinating story, but unfortunately that is all it is – a story.

The truth is that Andy Connell, a Gordon's Bay resident, found the cave. As children came along, Andy and his wife thought up the tale, and built the cairned grave with its wooden cross. As their children grew up the tale of Herr Rudy was told to them, and thus enthralled, the children would visit and stay at the cave with Mum and Dad.

There came a time when the children – now adults – were told the truth. That must have been similar to finding out there isn't really a Father Christmas. Sad to think that leaving childhood is sometimes a spoiler of imagination.

The Hermits Cave
Curiouser and curiouser. Of all the HH Rim caves I have explored, the caves of the spine - N2 to the sea - remain the most intriguing. Somewhere high up on the spine lies what we call 'The Hermits Cave'. Amongst all the caves, this one is one of the most difficult to find. There is a good reason for this – it has been deliberately camouflaged!

Unlike the De Landrost Hof the Hermits cave has no definite story, but the very fact that currently we have no idea who constructed the cave, makes it all the more interesting.

Some time ago someone came across a jumble of rocks, and realised that with a little bit of work, it could become a nice, liveable little hideaway. It must have been over a period of some time, that he and or she, toiled up here, day after day, carrying up Perspex windows to let into the gaps in the rock. The windows in turn were then sealed and made weather tight by applying expanding foam. A small stove was set in place, with a metal stove pipe reaching up to a hole cut into a piece of sheet steel covering a section of the roof.

There is a table with mugs, and cooking utensils in place, and room to sleep three quite comfortably. It is a long rough hike to get there, and all food and water would have to be carried in.

The cave entrance itself has been camouflaged with a door cut to the shape of the entrance, and coloured the same shades as the surrounding rock.

There is a story that the person who built and sealed the cave, used to visit the Gordon's Bay Library. Then armed with a selection of books, he would set off up to his mountain retreat, carrying water and supplies. Whoever it was also had a taste for wine, judging from two dusty empty bottles that we found.

This so far unknown gent would then stay in his 'cave' until he had read all his books, or until he ran out of supplies, whatever came sooner.

Looking at the weathering of the door, and the general 'feel' of the inside, we are guessing that the cave was made watertight around 20 to 30 years ago, and that it has not been used for some ten years or so. Scratched into the wall is the date '1990'.

If anyone could let me know of the cave's history, I would love to know more. Perhaps the unknown builder has left this life, and has left us a puzzle that which we may never be able to solve.

Stove with flue pipe.

The last 'throw' of the ridge

Access to the ridge end is problematical. One obvious entry point is via the Crystal Pools hike. However, this necessitates obtaining a Crystal Pools permit, the difficulty of which is similar to finding gold dust – I do understand the need to control numbers, though I do miss the times when we could just pitch up and hike. Once you have your permit, one is tempted to go on up to the pools, rather than explore off trail, which is discouraged anyway.

Final Ridge summit from Crystal Pool trail. 2.5B
Red. Indicating some exposure, with considerable amounts of easy scrambling. Five hours returning the same way. Only for the experienced, especially if using the upper watershed link and descent from the highest pool.

Ascents from the Crystal Pools trail begin at the section of the trail that climbs up over the first incline. Turning left leads to steep off trail scrambling, an enterprise frowned on by the authorities. If you do try to ascend from this side, be prepared to take on some loose ground, and navigational challenges to find your way round ribs and scarps of rock. Two hours will see you on the ridge, with its final summit just a short way to your left.

For the confident and experienced, it is now possible to traverse diagonally far right along and then down the hillside to pick up the watershed jeep track for 100m before turning right to pick up the Crystal Pools hike

A fine 'Eye on the skyline of the Stegasaurus ridge clearly seen from the upper sections of the Crystal Pools hike. Pic by Stu Summerfield

The last section of the HH Rim before it drops down to the sea

back from the upper high pool. The descent of which is loose in places and requires route finding ability. A wrong turn will put you above some serious drop offs.

An alternative is to gain the ridge from the Clarence Drive side. Though again this means very rough 'off trail' hiking and scrambling, and again is frowned on by the powers that wish to restrict our mountain access to known and accepted trails.

Ridge access via Filtration plant road to ridge end
Grade 3C Orange 5 hours return. Rocky scrambles on the ridge proper.

It is possible to use one of the lay-bys on the coast road and follow the first section of the road to the filtration plant. Cutting off the road at the very obvious bend. A gully now leads up to the ridge proper. This slope is steep and loose especially on descent. However, this entry point is useful for those wanting a long day, as they may then cross the watershed above the Crystal Pools, and on to climb Steenbras peak above.

From this entry point, once on the ridge, it is possible to follow the ridge directly with sections of scrambling, or skirt the tops just below the ridge on the east side, until it reaches its conclusion.

Ridge access via Clarence Drive to ridge end
Grade 2.5B Orange. Sections of easy scrambling still remain on the ridge to gain its end.

This alternative ascent is from further along Clarence Drive, utilising one of the parking / viewpoints. Ascend the more amenable open gully, easier on its right flank, to gain the ridge

The auther poses on the summit at the very end of the Hottentos Holland Rim

above. Follow the rocky ridge to its spectacular conclusion as it plunges down to the sea.

It has been a privilege researching and exploring the rim, and my deep thanks go to those who gave of their own memories, which has done so much to make this guide more complete. Also, thanks to those who encouraged me on this journey, when I often doubted it would ever end. Thanks also to those estates that have given me access to their treasured places.

The journey has taken us around the rim, past many mountain tops, beautiful places, mysteries, trails, paths, caves and legends. But now the Hottentots Holland Mountain rim dips, almost regretfully into the sea. But the journey is not over - Let the next one begin.

Khoekhoe Rock art
Hottentots Holland Rim to the Cape

The oldest known rock paintings in the world are approximately 45,000 years old, and are found where they have been preserved in Indonesia and in underground limestone caves in Western Europe. There is no doubt that as Homo sapiens spread over the world with a shared need for self-expression, various art forms were developed, including rock paintings, carvings and engravings in a variety of subjects and designs.

The earliest Palaeolithic (stone age) art forms in Europe showed mainly animals with few human representations, but the oldest art in Indonesia includes hand stencils, animals, humans and simple geometric shapes.

In southern Africa, the oldest dated paintings come from Namibia at around 30,000 years ago, and are of animals on small portable slabs of rock. By contrast the oldest engravings on pieces of ochre from Blombos cave near Still Bay are in a geometric pattern and date to about 75,000 years ago

Painting style and age:
Examples of San rock art

Cederberg rock art. Photo Steve chadwick   *Aurora cave art.*

San and Khoekhoe art styles.
South Africa was no exception in this need for artistic expression.

In the south-western Cape there are several thousand sites with rock paintings in two groups. The older of the two has been called the 'fine line tradition' in which the paint was applied with a brush or feather or perhaps sometimes a porcupine quill. It was the work of San hunter-gatherers whose ancestors have lived in the region for tens of thousands of years. The paintings that still survive on the walls of rock shelters are probably less than 10,000 years old. They are mainly of human figures, as well as animals like the eland that were important in their belief system.

The more recent 'finger-painting' tradition in which the paint was applied mostly with a finger or broader brush, was made within the last two thousand years by the Khoekhoe herders. The paintings in this tradition are mostly in the form of geometric pattern made with dots and lines, and sometimes with handprints and a few animals and humans. The Khoekhoe introduced a new economy with domesticated sheep and cattle from eastern Africa to this part of the Cape about two thousand years ago.

Rock art colours:
The most common shade of paint was made from red ochre, but yellow ochre was also used. White paint was made from bird droppings or shades of white clay. White was possibly also made from ostrich eggshell which was ground to a powder. Black was made from charcoal and manganese oxide.

The binding / mixing medium might be egg white , plant juices, fat, milk or animal blood. 'Ochre (pronounced OAK-er) is clay pigmented by hematite, a reddish mineral that contains oxidized iron, which is iron that's been mixed with oxygen' - Paul Pettitt, a professor of Palaeolithic archaeology at Durham University in the United Kingdom.

Because ochre is a mineral, it has proved to be the most enduring as it stains the rock. It also doesn't wash away or decay, allowing it to persist through the ages. 'It's vibrant colour and ability to adhere to surfaces make it an ideal crayon or paint base,' April Nowell, a Palaeolithic archaeologist and professor and chair at the Department of Anthropology at the University of Victoria in Canada.

Which is why most of the rock art we see today is red. This is true for all rock paintings throughout the world.

Reasons for rock art
This discussion had been and will continue to be debated for many years. In the 1950's one proposition was that it was 'art for arts' sake'. In other words - done for fun as a casual pastime.

This theory has now been discredited, and the current belief is that most of the rock art, like paintings in a church, depicts rituals, symbols of power, and traditional beliefs.

Traditional healers for example, were taught how to induce an altered state of consciousness, or trance, to receive power from the spirit world that would enable them to heal the sick. The ritual is recognisable in many paintings.

This explanation was given weight thanks to research amongst the San people whilst their traditions were still strong. It is possible to identify in the rock paintings the postures that healers take when receiving power from their ancestors. Animals like the eland help healers to get close to the spirit world.

The rock was considered a portal from this life to the life in the spirit world where the healer received spiritual power and guidance.

Area of Khoekhoe Rock Art
In this narrative we are looking for traces of rock paintings in the relatively small area of land between the Hottentots Holland Mountain Rim and Cape Point. It was here that some of the European seafarers landed briefly from the 16th century onwards, and recorded meetings with the Khoekhoe herders when trading with them.

It is also in this area that archaeological evidence shows that the ancestors of the San hunter-gatherers have lived there from at least 70,000 years ago, and that they continued to do so even after the Khoekhoe herders became their neighbours about 2,000 years ago. Only a few rock paintings in this small area have been found, and all are in the 'finger' painting tradition.. However, beyond the Hottentots Holland Mountain Rim in the Wimmershoek and adjacent mountains, there are many examples of fine line paintings.

Vandalism
At this point I must make the uncomfortable proviso that I am not going to describe the location of two of these currently known finger-painting sites.

The Fish Hoek Peers Cave site is already well known.

Graffiti on the wall of Peers cave Fish Hoek.

The very fact that Peers Cave is known and is accessible has left it open to charcoal, spray paint and marker pen vandalism.

In 1924, Peers cave was excavated by amateur archaeologists Victor Peers and his son Bertie. Their work, plus later studies, lowered the floor of the cave by some 10m. Such that the level the artists stood at as they painted now lies 10m above the current cave floor, making access to the artwork impossible without a long ladder. For this resulting protection we must be grateful, for the lower level reachable cave wall has long since been vandalised.

What has happened at Peers cave is indicative of our greatest fear — that of vandalism wrecking examples South Africa's heritage and sacred places.

If you do know the location of the rock art sites 2 and 3, please be circumspect regarding passing this information on.

Site 1/ Peers Cave

Also known as Skildergat. This site lies on a south facing escarpment, easily accessible from the coast road by a short hike.

The rock art is typical of the other two local Khoekhoe art sites that we know of; that of finger daubs and some irregular lines.

We may only speculate as to their meaning and as to why they were painted where they were.

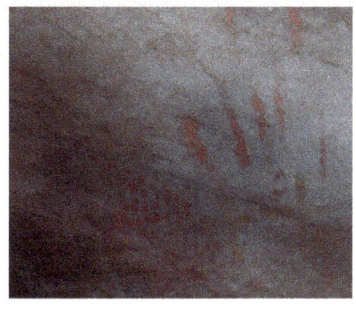

Rock art Peers cave Fish Hoek.

However, there is a strong feeling in academia that rock art is an expression of spiritual beliefs and therefore has symbolic meaning that is difficult to identify with certainty today.. The Peers Cave rock paintings were once thought to be the only example of rock art within roughly a 100-kilometre radius of Cape Town. Happily, we now know that this is not so.

They do however remain some of the most southerly examples of rock art in Africa, together with others near Hermanus and De Hoop.

Site 2/

This site lies within the rim of the Hottentots Holland mountains and has so far remained little known and protected due to its high and isolated location and difficult approach. It was recorded on a national database in the 1940s and was visited more recently by members of the S.A. Archaeological Society on the 11th of January 2015 and aided by information from the Mountain Club of South Africa.

Khoekhoe rock art at site 2, on the HH mountain rim

For the below narrative in italics I am indebted entirely to Dr Janette Deacon of the Archaeological Society:

'The paintings consist of two clusters of red dots probably made with a finger. The upper cluster consists of two rows of six dots…..the lower cluster has four horizontal and two vertical rows. Together there is a total of 48 dots with a possible third set, now barely visible at the bottom right.'

'This pattern is not typical of the naturalistic paintings attributed to San (Bushman) hunter gatherers who lived throughout southern Africa for many thousands of years. Dots like these were most probably made instead by Khoekhoe herders (pronounced Khwe-khwe, meaning 'people'), the people formerly called Hottentots by early European visitors and settlers at the Cape. Ancestors of the Khoekhoe originated in eastern Africa and migrated slowly southwards with domesticated sheep, reaching the Cape around 2,000 years ago.'

Several theories have been put forward for what the finger dots might represent. Counting is one possibility. Others believe they represent flashes of light that people see when they go into a trance. Another suggestion has come from Dr Jeremy Hollmann who has made a persuasive case for identifying them as representations of gifts given to girls during the Khoekhoe initiation ceremony. Published descriptions of girls' initiation rituals conducted in the 19th and 20th centuries describe the practice as follows. After her first menstruation, a girl would be taken by other women of the community to a pool or river. Her body would be covered with red ochre and clay to cleanse it. The clay was then taken off her body and placed in a leather bag. Sometimes the pelvic bones from a female sheep or goat slaughtered for the occasion would be placed in the bag as well. The bag was then thrown into the pool together with buchu and other sweet-smelling herbs. If the bag sank into the water, the people believed the Watersnake was happy with the girl and she would lead a peaceful life. However, if the bag did not sink it was a sign that the Watersnake did not approve of her.

After a positive message there was celebration with dancing and singing and the girl would receive many gifts such as necklaces of ostrich eggshell and shell beads, and aprons made of leather and decorated with beads. The patterns of beads decorating these gifts are similar to the patterns of dots on the rock shelter wall that is situated close to a pool in the river. We know from historical records that Khoekhoe groups lived in this area (hence the name Hottentots Holland) and it is very possible that the dots mark a place where a girls' initiation ceremony took place.'

Dating the paintings is difficult. The Khoekhoe could have inhabited the area from as early as 100 AD. It is sometimes possible to date a site from the type of stone tools in the adjacent area, but currently no trace of stone tools has been found. Artefacts may have existed, but regular spate flooding of the local stream in the area around the base of the paintings wall would have scoured the area of any such tools. Such that we are left with conjecture and may only guess that ceremonies took place at this remote site at any time from a few hundred to around 1,900 years ago.

After several visits over the years I still approach the site with a feeling of reverence. This place had a strong spiritual meaning to those who left us but a tantalising record of their presence some hundreds of years ago.

A white canvas for a khoekoe artist a long time ago.

Site 3/

Also located within the Hottentots Holland Rim is a chance discovery I made whilst guiding a group up a trail. The site had lain hidden for hundreds of years, and would have remained hidden but for a recent veld fire that cleared away thick proteas that had previously grown in front of the rock face. Even then it was a chance glance off the trail, followed by insatiable curiosity.

Not painted near flowing water, but near a pass where people and animals found a way through the mountain chain. It is possible that temporary camps were made nearby whilst cattle were being herded, or during seasonal migration of people to better grazing grounds.

In an area that is entirely made up of grey rock faces, one cannot help but conjecture that this isolated white rock face seemed to be irresistible to people camping nearby or just passing through who wanted to leave a mark of their presence.

This was in an age when carnivores happily hunted humans as well cattle. Perhaps this artwork was a spiritual offering for safe passage and protection from many predators, or was it a map of the best route?

Conclusions:
Are there more sites we do not know of?

Logic would say that although we only know of three HH Rim to Cape Point Khoekhoe rock painting sites; there must be more.

Site 2 may have served as a ceremonial place for the whole of the Helderberg basin. A special place, unique in the area and not duplicated.

Over the years the area has been well explored by members of the Mountain Club of South Africa, who always find caves interesting, but so far no more rock art sites have been reported.

Site 3 is near the summit of a natural route through the mountains that we know was used by the Khoekhoe, long before Europeans arrived. But……sites 2 and 3 are not in caves. Site 2 is on a leaning wall, whilst site 3 is on an open rock face. Perhaps we are looking in the wrong places?

Closeup of right panel. More finger daubs and some irregular shapes.

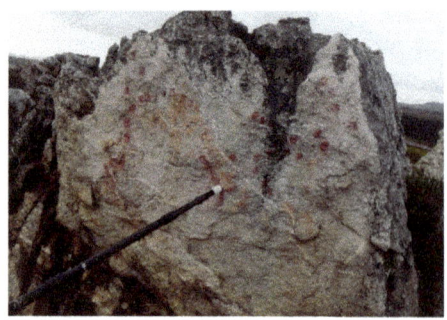

Why are the Khoekhoe paintings so 'symbolic' and the San images so 'artistic'?
The answer probably lies in the reasons for making paintings in the first place. If we accept that rock art worldwide reflects the beliefs of the people who made it, rather than the food they wanted to eat, both symbolic and naturalistic images will send a meaningful message to members of the same belief system. Symbolic representations of items associated with Khoekhoe initiation ceremonies are just as powerful to people 'in the know' as the symbolism associated with San hunter-gatherer trance healing. To use the Christian analogy, a symbol of the cross will send the same message to believers as a painting of Jesus on the cross.

It might seem as if the Khoekhoe were far less prolific artists than the San, but we need to take into account that they only lived as herders in the part of South Africa for less that 2,000 years. Whereas the San rock art tradition stretches back over 30,000 years.

It would be interesting if we were able to date our local Khoekhoe artwork. Unfortunately, the ochre-based paint used by the Khoekhoe does not seem to contain enough organic ingredients to make the radiocarbon, or Carbon-14 dating method possible. It is a pity that they did not make finger paintings in black with charcoal for the pigment

So many questions we do not know the answers to.
One thing for sure, when we are up on those hills we will, as always, keep our eyes open.

"Africa's rock art is the common heritage of all Africans, but it is more than that. It is the common heritage of humanity." Nelson Mandela

Grateful thanks to the following References:
1/ Dr Janette Deacon. "Personal communication".
2/ Dean Liprini. "Personal communication".
3/ https://sanbona.com/the-rock-art-of-sanbona-wildlife-reserve/
4/ https://www.sahistory.org.za/article/grade-5-term-1-hunter-gatherers-and-herders-southern-africa
5/ https://www.kaggakamma.co.za/news/index.php/2017/09/15/khoikhoi-tale-real-people/
6/ https://www.smithsonianmag.com/smart-news/new-technique-shows-san-rock-art-5000-years-old-180962948/
7/ Human Origins Research South African Journal of Science 99, May/June 2003
8/ Mary Lange – Water Stories and Rock Engravings- Eiland Women at the Kalahari Edge
9/ http://www.africanrockart.org/danger/vandalism.html
10/https://www.google.com.gh/search?source=univ&tbm=isch&q=peers+cave+rock+art&sa=X&ved=2ahUKEwj3otKKiuXyAhXKTsAKHa6FBKQQjJkEegQIChAC&biw=1199&bih=712
11/ https://economictimes.indiatimes.com/magazines/panache/art-from-the-past/articleshow/72615670.cms?utm_source=contentofinterest&utm_medium=text&utm_campaign=cppst

Thanks also to the Helderberg Estates for allowing access. Never taken for granted

Running the Rim

Looking through my mails, I came across a note from a friend with a map showing the dream of a hike / run from Crystal pools to West Peak.

Access: Due to Water authority restriction, CN trail closures and illegal off trail running 90% of this route is currently off limits. I do not write this to encourage folk to run the rim, but merely to note it for posterity, for those of us who dream that one day we might be able to hike or run it.

The Rim from the N2 to HNR West Peak has been attempted several times and apparently completed only once - post Boland by a MCSA team of four - in a midnight to 21:00hrs epic. Running or hiking the entire rim from Crystal Pools area to West Peak, to my knowledge, has never been done. Pre Boland, I don't think the full rim from N2 was ever accomplished.

A little history - 1932
The oldest record we have is of a trip by an MCSA party – H. V. Begley, L. Thresher, B. Cameron and R. Kingma, who made a three-day trip in 1932 – well pre Boland trail. Leaving Sir Lowry's Pass around 15:00, they ascended a gully right of Hans si Kop. They then climbed that summit and went on down to bivvy on the nek below.

The next day they climbed Moordenaarskop, and on to the tops of Langkloofberg and Langkloofpeak, and on up Vallieberg.

Bad weather put them off course such that they missed climbing Landdroskop, but went on to climb Sneeukop, which they reached around 17:15. The Triplets were next, and the team were on the top of the middle and highest triplet at 1,515m, time 18:10.

After taking in the third Triplet, the team descended out of the wind, to camp below a rock band at 18:30.

The next day the four went down a steep gully to arrive at the top of Diepgat, and on up to reach Pic Sans Nom 1,162m by 12:15.

Rain now set in, so the team descended down into the Jonkershoek valley. Certainly, an epic for the time. Courtesy of the MCSA 1932 journal.

Looking along the Rim from high on the south east ridge of Haelkop.
Pic courtesy Wouter van den Heever.

Section 1/ Crystal pools to the N2
13km. Grade 3.5C Red. 6 to 7 hrs. With slow going as you scramble along the initial serrated ridge, and a long walk out along the old dam access road.

Despite passing near the Steenbras dam, there is no water en-route, unless you drop down the few 100m from the walk out road to the reservoir itself.

There is a strong security fence in place all round the entrance to the Crystal Pools trail entrance. I remember way back when one did not have to book at all. Frustrated people were apparently digging under the old less robust fence when they couldn't get a booking - I am not condoning this one way or the other, I just record history.

From the Crystal Pools gate, hike as far as the first climb left of the stream, then as you reach the top of the short rise, turn left directly up and ascend past several right to left rising rock bands. I have made this hike several times, not difficult as you weave about through the rock. You come out just right of the furthest southernmost point of the rim at height 415m, where the ridge finally drops down into the sea.

Alternatively, you may also reach this point by being dropped off by the roadside and climbing the west side of the ridge via a wide though somewhat loose gully that rises up left of the nose of the ridge. This obviates the need to enter the Crystal Pools trail.

Steve C in 'Eye' one of the several Dinosaur ridge undulations. Pic courtesy of Brad Roe

From here the traverse begins. Hidden just behind the second top, only some 100m distant is the curious 'Hermits cave' complete with camouflaged door and watertight windows; with room to sleep three.

Because of its undulations, this section of the Rim is known as Dinosaur ridge, though it is so jagged that it could be called Stegosaurus ridge. Direct, the ridge is very time consuming involving several sections of scrambling, but all passable on the right 'east' side. before gaining the water plant, which you would need to bypass.

Access to the ridge from here to the N2 is not allowed by local bylaw, so you would be 'trespassing'.

Provided that you could get past this area, you would pick up the old road from the works to the dam itself. Follow this until it zig zags down to the dam. Then pick up the old dam access road that goes right along to the N2. Survey maps show this very well.

To follow the ridge when the old road is just a 100m or so below you is not really practical. I once climbed up to the ridge from the GB sign, with intent to follow the ridge to the N2. I soon dropped down to the dirt road and followed it to the N2 - it's still a long way. The gate at the exit to the N2 is manned, but it is possible to turn left just before you reach it, to come out at the top parking viewpoint. This negates having to walk out past the manned gate hut. Trails runners I know using this road have been hauled off to the water authority offices and threatened with prosecution.

Section 2/ N2 to the Noodskuiling Boland Refuge.
17km. Grade 4C Red. 7 to 8 hrs. Several sections of this trail are still in excellent condition. No water until reaching the east flank of Moordenaarskop, where several streams tumble down. There is also a stream beside the Noodskuiling refuge.

Starting from the N2 allows you to get dropped off at the viewpoint and cross the busy road to gain the old 1830 road, which takes you along to the Boland trail past the left turn to the old 'Gantouw' pass.

You can begin a little lower at the lay-by below the rail line, but you then have a climb up crossing the rail line to the higher jeep track. Risky security at the lay-by, though folk do park there.

Follow the jeep track past point 631m, then turn left, back on yourself to pick up the Boland. You can turn up to the 'Gantouw' and turn right to the Boland from there, but the linking ground is rough and would add another half an hour to what is going to be a long day.

Once on the Boland the going is good, as the trail is still in remarkably fine nick in this area. Onwards to gain a high point just below hill marked as 838m; from where you descend somewhat to pick up the tarred road that leads up to Hans se Kop - to use one of its four names.

Then it is a grind up the tarmac to gain Groot Waainek. Very rare to be seen by anyone as the maintenance crew only use the road to check equipment about once a week.

Hans se Kop from the north whilst on the Boland trail showing the spiral road up to the comms towers.

The Boland, clearly seen, climbs up from Klein Waainek taking in several rock steps. Pic courtesy of Stu Summerfield

*Settling down on the floor of the old 'Noodskuling' refuge.
Pic courtesy of Stu Summerfield*

Strictly speaking of course CN have banned access to this section of the Boland. We are campaigning for its reopening.

The path is again still in good nick but begins to deteriorate as you gain height along the south east flank of Moordenaarskop.

There are several zigzags up the side of the hill, but nowhere hectic. During my trips there over the last few years we have tried to do a little clearing whilst 'on the move' but the flora is fast gaining ascendancy. The way flattens out as you contour round to meet the old 'escape route' that climbs up from Buys se Pad way below to the South east. We marked this point with a cairn. Water available from several streams on this section

The feint trail now swings west to drop down a little into Klein Waainek, which lies at the top of Katjiesboskloof.

The way now climbs diagonally up to cross several rocky steps, easy enough but tricky in the wet with some exposure. There are several feint sections mixed with very clear sections where you can really motor on, until you reach the flank of Langkloofberg 1,338m.

The Boland now swings left into a distinctive 'V' kloof. With the Noodskuiling refuge some 100m up on the left-hand flank of the kloof.

The refuge once sported walls and a roof, but all was burnt down during one of the cyclical fires that swept through in years gone by. Now there are only two rock walls forming a semi sheltered corner, and a sloping concrete floor. Enough to sleep four if they are friendly.

If you wanted to take in the tops you pass on the way, then that's an even longer ball game.

Section 3/ Noodskuiling to Diepgat Nek.

18km using the Landdroskop hut loop. Grade 4B Orange. 7 to 8 hrs. Several sections of still excellent trail, but also contains the most difficult sections to follow.

Water at the stream near Guinevere, and at several hillside stream runoffs.

Mixed trail sections take you to the scree slopes south east of Valleiberg 1,385m. Here the Boland makes a sudden easterly turn, then back north to the marsh flats of Guinevere. This section is the most difficult in terms of overgrown trail vegetation - still possible to see, but tricky. Wild and great impressive scenery. How can this trail not be a national treasure!

A party 'running the rim' would now have a choice. Follow the Boland around to the huts, then up the westerly trail from the huts up to the nek above Landdroskloof (this trail is 'another' currently closed by Cape Nature) - or - from Guinevere directly north, off trail, over the Nek west of Landdroskop 1,515m to descend and again to pick up the Nek above Landdroskloof. Perhaps 1/3 the distance, but off trail bundu bashing.

The trail north from the Nek is remarkably good, though unrelenting as it climbs diagonally up round the east flank of Somerset Sneeukop 1,590m. The highest by 1m in all the Hottentots Holland mountain range, Victoria Peak being 1,589m.

Contouring below Valleiberg towards the screes below point 1,368 m. Pic courtesy of Stu Summerfield

The trail heads north past the Triplet, along the very same way used by those tough men who set up the triangulation beacon on top of Sneeukop back in 1844. One man died due to hypothermia on a resupply climb up Kurktrekker to the summit station.

Again, ignoring the summits of the Triplets to your left, you will descend slightly to pick up the Swartboskloof trail, which is followed via some great scenery and undulations to reach the nek of Diepgat; that impressive slash that cleaves the Hottentots Holland mountain rim.

Guinevere's field

Path junction with the way across to Sneeukop and the Landdroskop hut. Link now currently closed.

Section 4/ Diepgat to Haelkop summit
7km using the ridge direct to Haelkop. Grade 4C+ Black. Possibly the most intimidating and difficult section of the 'Rim'.

No water on this section unless you take the option to drop down the Swartboskloof trail. You would then swing left to traverse the Sosykloof contour until the central trail comes up from below, where 100m further you will find an old trail heading up diagonally left. This is feint in its upper section, but reaches the top of a wooded glade before traversing up and left to reach an obvious break in the cliffs, just below the nek at 1,015m, with Haelkop south east ridge above. This variation would add 2 to 3 hours to your trip

View looking north west from point 1,191, above Diepgat. Pic courtesy of Wouter van den Heever

Typical blocky descent on the Diepgat to the Nek 1,015 m ridge. Pic courtesy of Wouter van den Heever

Looking back down the early section of the Haelkop south east ridge. The ridge to Diepgat (hidden) beyond Nek 1,015 m. Pic courtesy of Wouter van den Heever

Taking the ridge direct from Diepgat to the nek below Haelkop at 1,015m.

This linking ridge looks innocuous from below, but is in reality very serrated with several towers that must be taken direct or with variations to the right. Certainly, scrambling ability is required with a head for heights. Sections of this ridge have been cairned to show the best line. Word from ascensionist's is that if you reach a 'sheer drop off', back track and go down to take a lower traverse. There is always a way through.

Final section of the south east ridge to Haelkop beacon.

The ground from the nek at 1,015m to the summit of Haelkop provides for some rock steps and scrambling; with not great difficulty.

Section 5/ Haelkop to Grootnek
6km Grade 2.5B Orange. Time 3 to 4 hours. There are some tricky descent sections.

No water on this section unless you drop down to the marshy stream east of Suurberg.

Top of Suurberg 1,092 m. Pic courtesy of Wouter van den Heever

Descending the west ridge of Haelkop 1,384m, provides some scrambling but nowhere hectic.

The ascent of Haelkop has become an issue. Easiest way was to climb up past the CN offices in Jonkershoek, but CN have stopped recent parties from this route. Many now ascend from Paradyskloof via the steep west side of Stallenboshberg, then cross east to bivvy by a stream for the night. Climbing Haelkop the next day and returning the same way. It is a long hike, maybe grade 4.5 to 5 if tried in a day.

Let the traverse continue. As you descend the west ridge of Haelkop, it begins in its lower section to swing south east and flattens out in a rounded ridge that leads across to Suurberg 1,092m. As part of the rim traverse there is no actual need to top out Suurberg, but rather swing south to pick up a long ridge that continues the 'Rim'.

Descending the ridge to Grootnek.

I have cairned this ridge to show the easiest line, but more importantly to show where to turn right, off the ridge, to down climb the flank. The ridge itself ends abruptly at a steep buttress, which is best avoided. Follow the cairns down the right flank and pick up the top of a left to right gully that takes you through the rock band. Now it is just a steep down slope descent to reach the nek before the ridge to Grootnek.

From this point, there is an escape down to your right

to pick up a feint trail that leads down to a long kloof filled with huge boulders. Then on down the lower wooded kloof to pick up the estate road at the head of Paradyskloof.

For the traverse, continue south west along the broad ridge in front of you, overcoming several minor tops, and rock steps, before descending the steep open slope down to Grootnek. This is the nek that provided an alternative early route for settlers wishing to travel from Stellenbosch to Somerset West, without having to swing round Cape Flats, with its difficult sandy terrain.

Section 6/ Grootnek to West Peak
10km Grade 4C Red. Time 6 to 7 hours. Difficult route finding. There are some tricky ascent / descent sections. Time includes finishing at HNR gate but excludes climbing minor peaks between Driekop and the Dome, and the two tops between the Dome and West Peak.

No water, though a support party could meet the traverse party; or food and water could be preplaced at Grootnek, 529m.

Looking back along the 'Rim' from the summit of the Dome. Pic courtesy of Brenda Marx

A well-maintained estate road now swings right, then back left to cross the spur above. At this point you would have to leave the road and turn up and take on the challenge of the slope above. There is an old trail that runs right to contour the hill, but doesn't really take you in a direction that the rim traverser wants to go.

I have not done this section, and as such, my arrows on the pic above are purely conjecture. Talking to those who have descended this section, all agree that this is the most problematic in descent. At least by going up, you would have the advantage of seeing where you might go.

Apparently, once through the lower rock bands, the way becomes easier until reaching the Dome.

There are three separate tops – Dreikop 971m, point 935m and point 882m before reaching the Dome at 1,137m.

Descending the Dome should be known home territory, but this descent is famous for folk turning right too soon. Directional care must be taken on this descent. Assuming that you might by this time be totally exhausted, climbing the two minor peaks between the Dome and West Peak could be two tops too far. So, it's the final well-known clamber up the north east ridge of West Peak. Where I will be waiting with a bottle of champagne!

Notes:
My sections do not necessarily indicate day portions. They are just convenient delineations.

Previous ascentionist's:
Circa 2015. Wouter Van den Heever and Danie Cilliers made a trail running traverse from Jonkershoek gate, up Swartboskloof, on past Sneeukop, along the Boland to the N2. Starting early morning, and finishing at the N2 around 15:00. So around nine hours.

Circa 2016 Also leaving at Jonkershoek gate Wouter and party again ascended the Swartboskoof trail, but this time turned right to take the ridge between Diepgat towards the 1,015m nek before ascending Haelkop. They then ran on along the Stellenboschberg ridge and so on down to Stellenbosch. Time around 8 hours!

Date unknown, but post Boland trail construction. It is reported that an MCSA trail running team of Lydia Roos, Andy Davies, Neil Pieter and Andre van Duran made the traverse starting from the N2 around midnight finishing at West Peak at 21:00. This remains the first and currently only circumnavigation of the rim. They are reported to have also taken in several main tops - research is ongoing regarding the actual tops they summited. In any event, an amazing achievement.

The Seven Tops run
The circuit from West Peak to Kliennek is known as the 'Seven Tops run'.

Mike O'Keefe and Brian De Villiers made possibly the first ascent circa 2002.
Time taken – 12hours.

More recently Brenda Marx and partner made the run in nine hours. Most serious scrambling

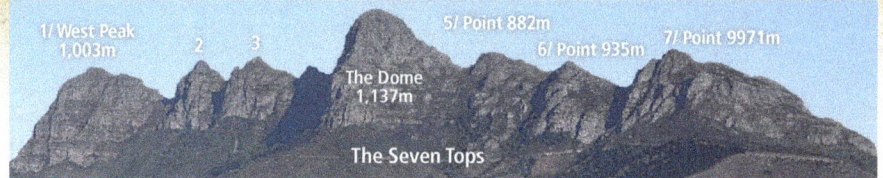

was encountered climbing the two minor peaks between West Peak and the Dome, and descending from Driekop to Grootnek.

Jonkershoek Horseshoe:

On pages 40/41 of his informative booklet on Jonkershoek (Jan 1982), Ernst Lotz describes the 'Die Jonkershoek Marathon', which is the horseshoe navigation of Jonkershoek. This begins with Bothmaskop and follow the ridge south east past the Twins, First Ridge Peak, Banghoek Peak, thence to pick up the Panorama trail round to the top of Kurktrekker. On round taking the Swartboskloof to the top of Diepgat, then continuing along the ridge to Haelkop and along the Stellenboschberg ridge to finally drop down the Stellenbosch. Apparently this massive trip has been accomplished a few times in one day. Ernst note the time as being around 11 ½ hours.

Looking back across to Driekop whilst decending from the Dome. Pic courtesy of Brenda Marx

Rock climbing routes on Hottentots Holland Rim

Upper south face of the Dome. Unclimbed? Would be 3 to 4 pitches.

Researching through MCSA journals, reading old notes sent to me, as well as interviewing 'older' MCSA climbers, has meant that I am dealing with grade definitions that span over a hundred years of exploration and climbing.

It is thought that Langklippie Ridge was first climbed in 1912 and repeated in 1921. Sadly, no written records were made of these ascents.

H. V. Begley, and party climbed Langkloofberg Face in Dec 1914, and left us a charming description of climbing a face that was a huge leap of faith for its day, however, they did not grade the climb.

It is true that by using a comparison chart of old and current grade systems, one may at least equate current grades, but given that they overlap, there is a risk of moving up or down a grade. Thus, I have, where it is given, retained the old grade. It is to be hoped that future ascents by climbers will update both grades and descriptions into the modern idiom, so that we may correct future guides.

As far as I have been able I have distilled the charming descriptions as given in old journals into our more modern parlance of route description. Again, these will need corrections by futures ascensionists.

Route and pitch lengths have been changed from Imperial to meters.

Descriptions working from left to right of the rim:

The Dome. South Face

There are stories, legends almost – of a party climbing this impressive face. There are no known details.

Access is difficult as traversing in from Helderberg Nature Reserve is off trail and frowned upon. This part of the mountain is Cape Nature, who also frowns upon off trail access. It is

Unclimbed pillar on the south east face of the Diepgat/Nek 1,015 m ridge.

not likely that permission would be granted to access directly up Lourensford or Erinvale.

Ridge - Nek 1,015m to Diepgat
This south-east facing scarp holds several towers that might hold interest for future climbers.

Pic Sans Nom
We have teasing historical notes but no details that the strong activist of the period G. Londt climbed a 'lovely E grade ridge' on the south side of Pic Sans Nom. Circa 1922."

Pisgah
Working on round the inner rim and passing Diepgat, the next face to catch the eye of a climber is the impressive Pisgah North wall.

Pisgah North Wall. Photo courtesy of Dante Visser

Access: Members of the MCSA may ask the club for permission. The club in turn will apply to Lourensford Estate. Be aware that unless permission is given to drive to the base of Diepgat, the climber faces a two-hour trek along the high jeep tracks left across to Diepgat.

The story of Pisgah North Wall
This rock-climbing addendum is not just a guide, it is a history, and thus it is also an effort to give due credit to climbers whose exploits for the period were exceptional and very bold.

The foot of the wall
Standing at the foot of a route with guidebook in hand is in some ways a comfort. You know that the grade should be within your climbing ability. It might even tell you where to place key protection.

You are about to play the game that climbers play the world over – you want that adrenaline rush of fear; but not to die, and a guidebook, aided by modern equipment, lowers that risk to manageable proportions.

In the past, I have been privileged to have partnered some exceptional rock climbers and mountaineers, whilst exploring and making 1st ascents. Such that in some ways I feel a link with the excitement and the fear that those early Hottentots Holland explorers would have experienced as they stared up at those towering unclimbed walls and ridges.

Imagine then, standing at the foot of Pisgah North wall with no guide. You don't know if it will be too difficult for you. Will there be protection to stop a big fall? Will there be loose rock? You may be at your best, confident and strong, yet, to some degree you will be afraid. Modern climbing ropes stretch up to 40% and help to absorb the force of a fall. You will also be wearing a climbing harness which will cradle your body.

Our predecessors had no helmets, they tied direct onto a hawser-laid hemp rope around their waist. This rope had little to no stretch. Fall far enough and it will break your back. A climber falling and ending up under an overhang, suspended in space has minutes before the blood supply to his lower body is cut off.

For climbers setting foot on unclimbed rock faces pre 1940's, with their hemp rope and a few slings complete with heavy metal karabiners, it was a huge leap of faith, with commensurate high risk. They had balls, including the women that sometimes climbed with them!

The early ascents of Langkloofberg Face route – 1914, and Pisgah North wall - 1922, remain as monuments to the early pioneers.

The geography of the Pisgah Ridge
The face of Pisgah seems from below to be an integral part of the Hottentots Holland mountain rim, but it is in fact detached from the mountains behind by a deep wide gully known as the Staircase. Descent from both of the following climbs would be down into the Staircase left to exit via Diepgat, or right to climb the shoulder and descend the gully and rocky stream bed of Sneeukopkloof. Chippaway cave up and left of Sneeukopkloof might be an option at the end of a long day. See directions in main text of guide.

Pisgah North face. Climbs the impressive wall right of Diepgat Ravine.

Pisgah North Wall. No grade or description. G. Londt, Norman McLeod. Circa 1922.
November 1936 saw S. le Roux, O. Shipley and Miss Joan Fothergill set out to attempt to make a second ascent; this time with the goal of completing a route description, and grading the climb.

Examination of the face indicated that reaching and following a steep right to left diagonal crack system seemed most feasible. This was achieved, but further ascent of the deep crack was found difficult, and after 60m the climb was abandoned. *'At a point marked 'A' we found the crack quite unclimbable due to the absence of holds and the poor quality of the rock'*. Retreat was started by 14:00, and due to the difficulty of finding good abseil points, the foot of the wall was only regained around 22:00.

Photo courtesy of Dante Visser

Further examination of the face using powerful binoculars indicated that the team should climb the centre of the face and then traverse right, into the diagonal crack and a point higher up the face, at a point marked 'C'.'

The second attempt to repeat the wall took place on the 21st November 1937. S le Roux, O. Shipley. Miss Fothergill being unable to attend.

Planning for a long day the two men reached the foot of the wall at 05:15. In the grey of the breaking dawn they, tied onto their hemp rope. A few slings were put over their shoulders and by 05:30 there was light enough to climb.

1/ 56m. The start followed a difficult 16m crack. Followed 120m of steep scrambling first by a right to left weakness then a left to right grassy shelf followed steep scrambling leading to a 'Green Shoulder' marked as 'B' on the diagram.

2/ 120m. From the 'Green Shoulder' the route lay up a diagonal broken recess, consisting of a series of vertical gullies and recessed faces, which lead to the start of the traverse below the red overhangs.

3/ The traverse right begins as a ledge 3m wide, but quickly narrows and eventually disappears 1m before the entrance to the main crack. A sensational but not difficult hand traverse allowed the completion of the traverse into the crack at point marked 'C'. Length of pitch not given.

4/ 12m. Ascend the crack for 12m to a prominent chock-stone and small stance.

5/ 10m. climb the crack for a further 10m to a good chockstone belay.

6/ 11m. Step onto the left face and climb moderate ground to reach a good stance at the back of a crack.

7/ 18m. 'E'. Climb the difficult vertical pitch above to reach an excellent tree belay.

8/ Above the tree the climb moved left out of the crack, which was not entered again. Continue upward for a 'hundred or so meters' climbing a series of difficult pitches, some being vertical and in sensational positions, until an 'unclimbable face' is reached. Length of pitch not given.

9/ 12m. Traverse left for 12m to reach a broad ledge and belay.

10/ 27m 'E' From the stance, climb a 12m crack, followed by a difficult 15m face.

11/ 'E' Climb a further 9m crack followed by ascending a very narrow ridge of rock. The pitch was certainly the most sensational of the climb, as there appeared to be a sheer drop of about 550m into the kloof below'. Length of pitch not given.

12/ 25m. Continue by crossing a small slope to the right, and ascend a final moderate 18m pitch.

13/ 30m. A final section of rock scrambling leads to the summit.

From the green shoulder, the climb is consistently difficult and exposed; however, good belays are available on every pitch. The rock throughout is sound, though there is accumulated debris on ledges.

Time for ascent – 12 ½ hours. One hundred years on from the first ascent - in respect - I raise my hat and drink a toast to Messrs Londt, McLeod, S. le Roux and Shipley. Also, to the Langkloofberg Face Route team of H. V. Begley, C. West, G. F. Traverse Jackson.

Descent was down to the Staircase', and so back down to the base of Diepgat

Edited from: S. le Roux and O. Shipley (1937) MCSA Journal pages 62 - 64

This highest wall on the HH Rim had to wait 54 years for a further ascent, when in 1991 Mark Berry and R. Price visited, determined to take a more direct line on Pisgah's North Wall.

Boulevard Sans Nom.
Grade 19 (by hardest pitch) 455m. Mark Berry. R. Price. 1991.

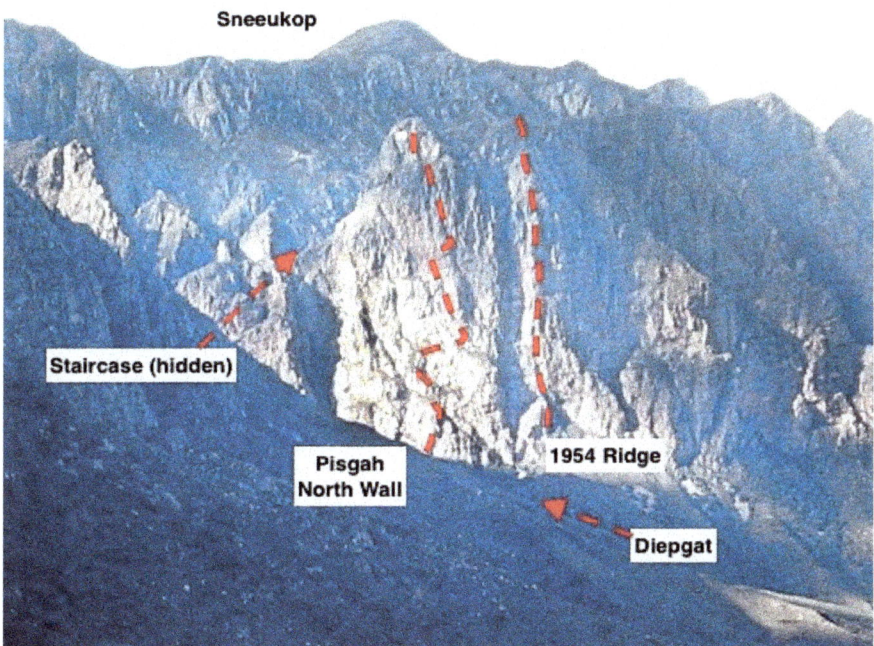

Approach: Follow the Diepgat outflow up from the dirt road for 40 minutes, then turn right to ascend a steep slope. Traverse left to scramble up water worn-rock until able to traverse diagonally right. Scramble up the steep rib above and move left to the start of climbing proper. Which is 5m left of a red 'dish' corner.

1/ 35m. 18. Climb a flake and groove with difficulty. Then climb diagonally left over water-worn rock to a ledge.

2/ 35m. 15. Move left and ascend an obvious corner crack and climb the left break up to a ledge.

3/ 40m. 19. Move up and traverse two meters left and continue up a 'tricky' face until it is possible to reach right for a flake to pull up on, and so up to a small stance.

4/ 30m. 18. Climb diagonally left to make a difficult move into a recess. Follow this up to a ledge, and traverse left to belay in the corner.

5/ 40m. 17. Climb 10m up the corner until it is possible to move right into another corner. Follow this to the top of a pinnacle, thence up to a stance.

6/ 40m. 14. Climb leftwards through a bulge and then carry on directly up to a stance.

7/ 40m. 13. Climb diagonally left towards the skyline and up a juggy wall.

8/ 40m. 14. Continue up the 'juggy' wall and move left to a small stance.

9/ 40m. 16. Climb steep rock above to traverse right and up to a commodious stance below a red corner.

10/ 40m. 15. Climb reddish rock to the left of a prominent corner to belay in a 'cubby hole'.

11/ 40m. 17. Exit left and climb the corner to its overhang. Traverse or dassie crawl right with some difficulty, then climb up to a large belay ledge beneath a shallow gully.

12/35. 15. Climb the face on the right to the right-hand corner, then diagonally left into a shallow gully which is followed to its top.

Scramble to the top of the buttress. Descend by traversing off the top towards Gordons Bay until it is possible to descend more directly to Trappieskloof, and so on down into Diepgat.

1954 Ridge. E
(12/13). V. Cheek, Arthur Doble. Nov 1953

From the old Picnic Bush site at the base of Diepgat, a ridge is visible between two ravines well to the right of the amphitheatres on the front of Pisgah. The ridge commences just to the right of the top of a large scree, partly covered by indigenous trees and has a prominent red nose-like overhang near its base. The route is well cairned.

1/ 'B' 30m. Up a short face followed by a shallow recess. The top of the pitch is in line with the red nose.

2/ 'C' 50m. Traverse right for 10m and then ascend a 40m gully.
3/ 'C' 12m. Up a small recess followed by a larger recess to the right to reach the crest of the ridge.

4/ 'B' 58m. Follow the line of the ridge crest. Belay as required.

5/ 'D' 21m. Climb the face of the ridge, followed by a 30m knife edge. Belay as required. Beware loose rock. Above this point the rock improves.

6/ 'C' 30m. Climb 'broken faces' bypassing a belt of overhangs on the right, and into a deep gully.

7/ 'E' 18m. Continue up the gully for 10m to a tree in a large cave-like overhang. Then traverse 2m right to reach the start of the 'E' section. Continue up the face for 4m and then work delicately right and continue upwards. The main climbing is now over.

Scramble up to the crest of the ridge and continue directly up in a series of direct straight forward pitches.

Sneeukopnaald

This fine pillar of rock rises imperiously for some hundreds of meters from the end of the Pisgah / Sneeukopnaald ridge. The climbing challenge of which was taken up by Michael Scott and Gabriel Athiros sometime in the mid 1970's. No route notes were made – tsk tsk.

Langklippiek & Langkloofberg

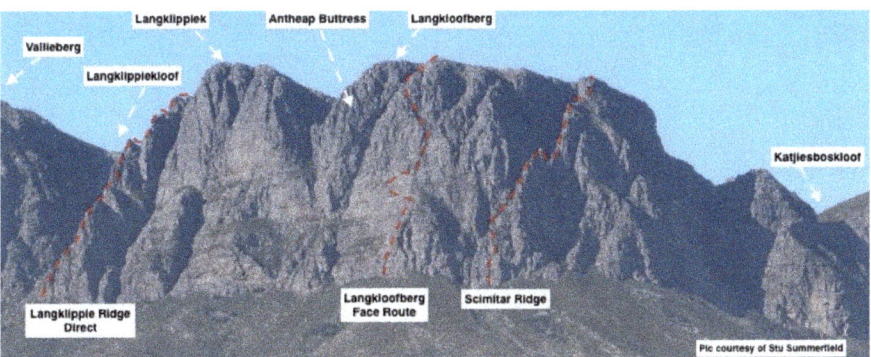

Photo courtesy of Stu Summerfield

Access: Members of the MCSA may ask the club for permission. The club in turn will apply to Vergelegen Estate. Park at Johnson Hut access point, and follow estate jeep tracks up right until bundu bashing is required to reach climbs.

Descents from climbs on Langklippiek would be north down into Langklippiekloof and thus back towards the Johnson hut. Exiting from climbs on the Langkloofberg, it would be possible to go south down into Katjiesboskloof left hand, but this would mean a long traverse back north beneath the 'Lang' piek faces to the hut. The better option would still be to cross the back of Langklippiek and descend Langklippiekkloof.

In a kloof on the east side, between the two 'Lang' pieks, just 100m up from the old Boland trail lies the site of the Noodskuiling refuge. The walls and roof were burned down during a fire, but the concrete floor is still useable as a bivy spot. Two sides are sheltered by short rock faces but you would still be exposed to any weather.

Of all the 'Inner Rim' peaks of 'The Rim', the western aspect of these two mountains contains arguably the greatest concentration of ridges and faces of interest to the climber, though due to their greater difficulty of access they have thus far not been explored as thoroughly as compared to the more accessible Jonershoek valley mountains.

Climbed in the early 1970's - South west face of Sneeukopnaald. Pic courtesy of Stu Summerfield

Exploration of this area began whilst looking for the line of least resistance of what has become known as 'Langklippie Ridge'. It is thought that some exploration was made during the latter part of 1912, but nothing is known of these very early forays.

The Ridge was climbed by R. Hallack and A. T. Prentice back in 1921, and again by G. Londt and Townsend in 1925 - great efforts for the time.

In November of 1934 W. M. Dodds and S. le Roux set off to climb the ridge by following the line of the early pioneers, and to reconnoitre the possibility of climbing the ridge by a more direct line up its serrated steps, exposed knife edges and steep tower faces. Their return in Jan 1936 resulted in:

Langklippie Ridge Direct.
E (11/12). M. Hallack, O. Shipley, W. M. Dodds, S. le Roux. Jan 1936

The route as reported in the MCSA journal does not give pitch by pitch details. So, the description below is an edited descriptive narrative from the journal. Thus, for repeating parties it becomes somewhat of an interpretive adventure. In keeping with such a historic line.

From the Johnson hut side head right and cross the bed of Langklippiekloof and ascend a short slope to the foot of the ridge which starts as a great broad rock buttress. Climb an easy crack of about 8m to a ledge at the base of a vertical pitch. From here traditionally the leader stands on the shoulders of his second to reach up to the right, where a short awkward traverse is negotiated using one reliable handhold.

From here, the climbing eases somewhat, though airy as the route now reaches the ridge proper, and becomes 'a true Knife Edge, with big drops on either side'.

Climbing a 9m face devoid of handholds is made easier by a convenient bush. (that we hope is still there – the climb was 86 years ago, Editor).

Above the wall, move right around a corner along a narrow ledge, 'then ascend over a good vertical drop to the top of the pitch'.

The climber now reaches the base of a large step in the ridge. Climb directly up the right side of the step for 13m, before a short traverse is made out to the skyline, the last part of which is a 'dassie crawl' under an overhang. Above this the climbing was made 'without difficulty', though the eye is ever more drawn by the steep crux as it rears above you.

A great tower of rock 90m high rises up from the gully on the south side, containing a large wall of yellow rock. High above, a prominent chimney is the goal.

Langklippiek Ridge itself joins the tower about 70m from its top, and at this point it is possible to escape left into the gully, but the direct line continues up with purity to climb the final section of the ridge.

Avoid the impressive face of the tower by climbing its left side on sound rock. Followed by a 6m diagonal traverse across to the centre of the face of the tower above the smooth wall, to reach a broad stance. A short exposed vertical pitch follows (take care at loose boulder) to reach a small belay 26m from the top of the tower.

Now follow a shallow recess which narrows to a crack – chock-stone belay at a commodious ledge, then climb without difficulty up a corner, with one long stretch to reach a small ledge at the base of the 10m chimney noted above. Climb the chimney via one awkward bulge, avoiding a jammed chock-stone at its top, by climbing the short face to its side. Above this the climbing eases off until the way is barred by a rock face some 10m high. There is a tantalising but loose flake which is avoided by a long reach and pull-up to the left. After which easing ground leads to the top. Descent was via Langklippiekloof.

Edited from: S. le Roux (1936) MCSA Journal pages 86 - 88

Next right are two buttresses, the lower sections of which are impressive walls that tail off into two separate ridges that reach up to the summit of Langklippiek. Both of which are currently thought to be unclimbed.

Right again are the ridges and faces of Langkloofberg. The left of which is nominally known as 'Antheap Buttress'.

Antheap.
F1 (13/14). Paul Anderson, Michael Scott. Nov 1971

Takes the inverted pear-shaped dome topped cone left of Langkloofberg Face and Scimitar Ridge. Ascent was made during a plague of ants – hence its name.

The climb's lower section is 'scruffy' but is 'compensated for by the superb break through the overhangs on jug-handles, and the clean crack system above'.
Edited from: Michael Scott (1972) MCSA Journal. Page 96

Langkloofberg Face
No grade given. H. V. Begley, C. West, G. F. Traverse Jackson. 16th Dec 1914.

A landmark climb for the period and probably the first 'rock climb' of significance on the inner rim of the Hottentots Holland Mountains.

Starting at the lower buttress directly under the summit, where a series of easy ledges lead diagonally right for 120m onto the face of the buttress on the right. From the top of the buttress a traverse left is made in the direction of a patch of white rock. The traverse ledge ends abruptly at a steep wall 14m high, which is ascended (crux) and passes the white patch. Traverse now to the right to reach a minor kloof which separates the main peak from a minor south peak. Ascend by crossing to the opposite shoulder, taking care of mossy rock in the kloof. Climb a corner formed by the shoulder via a tilted pavement of flat smooth rock finishing in a small chimney. Above the chimneys, easier climbing leads up on good rock to re-cross the kloof near its top. Traversing along a ledge leads to a pinnacle on the northern skyline. Climb the 10m crack formed at the junction of the pinnacle and the face, leading to a scramble to the summit.

Edited from: H. V. Begley (1914) MCSA Journal. Page 62-66

Scimitar Ridge.
Grade E. S. le Roux, W. M. Dobbs, 12th Mar 1939

Believed first climbed by G. Londt and N. McLeod, but no written record was made.

To the right of Face Route lie two high serrated ridges which form above two steep buttress faces. Both of which are also believed unclimbed. Right again is a deep kloof. Immediately right of the kloof is the fine line of Scimitar Ridge.

The broad base of the ridge is undercut, but 30m right of the overhangs is a partially detached 30m pillar. Climb 12m over loose debris behind the pillar before traversing diagonally left to a ledge and tree belay. Now climb the horizontal narrow ledge for 25m before a 9m recess is followed by an easier 5m wall leading to a belay 18m above the start of the climb.

Traverse 8m left past the overhangs face into a steep gully that leads up for 20m to a broad belay ledge. Now climb an 'awkward' 8m pitch followed by a dassie traverse. A further 15m of scrambling leads to the foot of the next steep pitch. Climb thin moves on the pillar above to reach a small stance. Climb the 4m recess behind the belay before an overhang forces a move left over an awkward traverse. Further delicate moves are made to reach good holds on the top of the face.

The ridge now lies back. Scramble 30m to reach a 15m rock face. Climb the crack on its left-hand side, past further easy rock to reach the base of a prominent pinnacle. Descend slightly to make a long traverse on the north side of the pinnacle. A further descent of 8m leads to a narrow neck – cairn.

Ascend the next 90m by broken rock up and left, before working back to the centre of the ridge again. Now follow a short gully past a chockstone. A further 4m crack is climbed to another easy gully which leads to the final face. Follow a break on the left-hand side before returning to the ridge proper. Here a final 7m face is climbed diagonally right, followed by a gully and scramble to the summit.

S. le Roux (1939) MCSA Journal. Pages 49-50

Hans se Kop West Face Gully
Grade 4D **Black**. 300m

1st known ascent Mike Reid, Richard Sales. 13th September 2022.

From the high point of the jeep track through the granite boulders above Idiom, strike up towards the face itself, via some rough terrain and vegetation until reaching the base of the upper of two slanting left to right lines of weakness. On the first ascent no rope

A view of the upper section of the West Face Gully, with the mountains sheer rock wall on the left

The magnificent West face of Hans se Kop shoeing the West Face Gully route

was used, though taking a rope is advised as the way is steep and exposed with scrambling on many sections. All major difficulties were bypassed on the right until finally the upper section eases back to a more friendly open slope.

Idiom Bouldering

Access: Currently allowed with good relations in place with Idiom.

Sport climbing on the fine granite boulders that lie on the hillside up and left of Idiom Restaurant. The guide may be viewed on: https://drive.google.com/file/d/1rS6G5yC1vH-cAylYX1GLHU9D2mZycWKW/view?usp=drivesdk

Gordons Bay

A recently issued Cape Town Reserves by-law (October 2020) states climbing is banned without 'authorisation'. Water board authorities have also taken a strong line with trail runners, hikers and scramblers. This would seem to affect the entire hillside on both sides of the ridge from the N2 to the sea.

Slab and right wall of Owl crag

Owl Crag'

Access: Waterboard authorities actively discourage climbing in this area. By-law noted above.

Laying high on flank of the ridge, and being directly above the right-hand side of the dam below 'Sweetwaters', the crag was often gazed up at by climbers who wondered at the possibilities for climbs on the only crag in this part of the ridge that looks to have faces and slabs worthy of investigation. It took a determined visit

Front face of Owl Crag

by a climber who accessed by the higher dam road, and abseiled down the crag.

Possibly a two-pitch + venue, currently unclimbed.

Surfside – Gordons Bay

Access: Waterboard authorities actively discourage climbing on this crag. By-law noted above.

For details see Western Cape Rock. Guide to Sports Climbing by Tony Lourens.

Seaside Crag

Access: Waterboard authorities actively discourage climbing in this area. By-law noted above.

Approached by parking at the same hairpin bend as for Surfside sports crag above. Walk south on a rising diagonal until you see the half-domed crag on the skyline.

The flat wall on the left is the sports slab. The brown recess has an F2 line climbed by Dion Tromp and partner. In the middle of the amphitheatre a white strip lies diagonally up the brown walls below the overhangs. Further right, the skyline has the easy angled frontal rib.

Central Route.
F2 (14). Dion Tromp, Mike Scott. 1997.

1/ 13. The base is mostly undercut or very steep blank rock, but just past a cave a tricky start up an angled slab gives access to a rightwards traverse line to the white stripe.

2/ 14. Moderate climbing now leads to below the overhang. Here a traverse left is made over a smooth slab and past an old nest. At a broken recess a bold pull up and move left is followed by a short steep wall (crux) to a ledge.

3/ 13. On the left a combination of crack and faces is followed to the top. Walk down the north side to reach the descent slopes.

Mike Scott (1998) MCSA Journal. Pages 143.

Approaching 'Sea Side' Crag. Photo Mike Scott

Streenbras West Face

Steenbras West Face
Edited from M. A. Loos (1961) MCSA Journal. Pages 100-103

Access: Under the same restrictions noted above.

At the southern conclusion of this section of the Hottentot Holland where it drops down into the sea from the final peak, there is an impressive rock face on the seaward western side.

Triangle Face Route.
16. M. A. Dennis, G. Loos. 1959.

The 'Triangle' will be found near the foot of the face some 70m left of the start of Slab and Overhang Route. The Triangle Face route itself starts on the horizontal ledge just above it, at an obvious break in the overhangs just above.

1/ 25m 11. Ascend a short face in the bottom of the break, to a small overhang. Traverse left from beneath the overhang onto a rib that leads to a narrow ledge 5m higher. Follow this ledge to the left for 4m and climb into a smooth corner. Traverse left out of the corner and continue upwards for a further 3m to where a traverse can be made to the right and a comfortable stance just above the corner.

2/ 30m 15. Traverse to the right for 6m to a rib on the far side of some shaky-looking blocks. Ascend this rib, strenuous climbing required to turn an awkward bulging section about halfway up. From the top of the rib, pull past a narrow overhang on the face above, and continue upwards to a broad sloping ledge about 19m higher. Scramble diagonally upwards to the right for 25m to a prominent patch of smooth, white rock on the face above the ledge

3/ 19m 12. Ascend this white face on the left-hand side, then traverse to the right for 5m. Continue upwards, negotiating three short awkward corners in quick succession, the last one being situated on the underside of a squarish leaning block. A pull-up onto this to complete the pitch.

4/ 19m 16. Traverse to the right past a small tree, then step onto an exposed nose. Continue round the nose on handholds alone until a mantle movement can be made onto the face above. Work left across this face into a wide, broken-up crack, which is followed almost to the top of the pitch. Near the top of the crack, step out to the left, before continuing upwards to a large sloping ledge. Scramble up the ledge for about 9m.

5/ 14m D. Ascend an obvious corner past a large tree to the top of the climb.

Slab and Overhang route.
D/E. H. F. Snijders, M. A. Loos. Nov 1959

Provides 180m of varied and enjoyable climbing. The climb begins approximately 90m left of Frontal Route where it is possible to climb up just left of a small overhang.

1/ 13m D. Ascend the weakness left of the overhang to a stance beside a large bush.

2/ 30m E. Work up the face to the right of the stance, into the bottom of a recess running diagonally up to the left. Ascend this recess until stopped by an overhang, then cross the steeply sloping face on the left to an airy position on a projecting nose. Continue upwards above the nose to a stance 8m above.

3/ 12m C. Scramble up easy rock to the right of the stance to a ledge running around the face of the mountain. Belay or fix protection and traverse right for 25m to belay.

4/ 12m C. Ascend an obvious crack to the next ledge. This same ledge may also be reached by a scramble starting 8m further right. The next two pitches lie up the slab and through the overhang that gives the route its name.

5/ 15m E. Ascend a break on the right-hand side of the slab and through the overhang, then step left across to a good stance 3m to the left.

6/ 10m. D. Chimney through a break in the overhang above the stance by an aloe 4m up.

Above the aloe move a metre to the right and ascend to a comfortable ledge.

7/ 8m. B/C. Start 1.5m to the right of the last pitch and scramble to a broad bushy ledge which marks the final sections of the climb. The next pitch starts from the ledge directly below a prominent clump of dark green trees growing on the face about 25m higher.

8/ 14m E. Ascend a broken-up crack which starts about 4m up the face, until it is blocked by a small overhang. Move out of the crack to the left and cross a smooth narrow face, using a good handrail just beneath the overhang, to reach a comfortable stance 1m to the left.

9/ 9m E. Cross the sloping slab to the right of the stance and ascend the exposed corner on the far side on small holds – delicate climbing. A further 3m of easier rock completes the pitch, which wends its way up to just below the patch of trees noted above. Now move upwards and to the left through the trees to where the next pitch starts in a low, closed-in recess.

10/ 6m E. Climb the right-hand wall of the recess and pull up onto the face above. Scramble 22m (C) to a ledge beneath the final band of rock.

11/ 9m C. Ascend an obvious crack to the left of a small overhang for 2m. On the level of the overhang, traverse left out of the crack and scramble up a sloping slab to the top of the pitch.

Steenbras Frontal Route.
C/D H. J. Ackermann, A. C. N. Malkin. 1949.
The original route on the face, and has proved popular over the years.

1/ 45m C. Start directly below a prominent reddish-brown overhang near the right-hand edge of the West Face. Climb directly up a sloping face to the red overhang, possible belay stance. Move left for 10m until the ledge ends abruptly over a considerable drop.

2/ 10m D. Starting with an exposed 'step over', traverse left to a stance beyond the end of the overhang.

3/ 22m C. Ascend 5m up the broken-up corner to the left of the overhang. Scramble 12m up the bushy sloping ledge above and ascend a short face on the right (5m C) to a sloping ledge that leads off to the right and so onto the crest of the ridge forming the right edge of the West Face.

4/ 12m. C. Ascend the sloping face on the left of the crest.

5/ 14m C/D. Continue up a shallow flaky recess on the crest of the ridge, which finishes on a broad bushy ledge which is a prominent feature of the upper part of the West Face.

Traverse left around this ledge for 30m to avoid the sheer face forming the crest of the ridge above the ledge.

6/ 19m C/D. Ascend an obvious corner to the left of the face. Then traverse back onto the crest of the ridge to scramble to the bottom of a wide grey recess.

7/ 45m B. A further 45m of scrambling leads to the summit beacon.

Steenbras Western Ridge.
Grade E. (10). Richard Smith, Noel van der Wethuizen. Circa 1983

Comfortable belay on Steenbras Western Ridge

General description: Starts just right of the first pitch of Steenbras Frontal Route (see pg 101 MCSA Journal 1961). Where the frontal route traverses out left to overturn the large square buttress, climb the recess corner on the right-hand side of the buttress. At the top of the recess traverse left onto the western Buttress.

Two further pitches gain easier ground and the top.

Descent: Scramble down overlooking Steenbras River, the key is a large folded crack that can be observed from the climb.

Steenbras Prow Buttress

Believed to lie on the right-hand (Northern) side of the West face of Steenbras mountain. Location to be determined.

The ascent from Clarence Drive takes about 20 minutes. Currently three routes terminating at the summit, and a three pitch 'E' which runs into the first route. B+ scrambling to the foot of the climb.

Fence Line. Grade ?. Nigel Peddie, Mary Peddie Date Sep 1987
Start from the car park on the north side of the river mouth and ascend beside the fence.

The climb commences at the right-hand end of a sloping grass ledge, near a prominent waboom, in line with the fence.

1/ E. 32m. The start is on the end of paler rock and runs straight up the face for 17m before moving diagonally left and up again following an obvious line to a small but secure stance.
2/ D. 13m. continue straight up for 13m to a wide grassy sloping ledge – a prominent feature on the mountain. Follow the shoulder of the mountain across the ledge, still in line with the fence, to the start of the third pitch in a bushy path below a big open book with a brown overhanging roof.

3/ E. 14m. Make 4m scramble brings one to a comfortable diagonal sloping ledge with good belay points. From the ledge the route moves onto a small prominent overhanging nose. Move to the corner of the nose and ascend, moving around the corner to the right, finishing on a wide-open sloping ledge under the brown overhang. Traverse right, down to the ledge 20m to the foot of an open book with a 3m crack on the right-hand side.

4/ D. 15m. climb the open book corner past an in situ blister bush, to the end of climbing. Easiest descent is down the broad gully starting to the north east of the peak and running down to the road on the north side.

Hawse Pipe.
C+. Nigel Peddie, Mary Peddie Date 1990

Exposed in places such that a 'Rope may be necessary'. Head up towards a prominent fissure on the right-hand side. Descent is by an easy gully to the south.

1/ B+. Ascend 8m on the left side of the fissure to a narrow horizontal crack – the 'Hawse Pipe. Remove packs to 'wriggle' through to the right for about 6m. This will bring you out onto the right shoulder of the buttress

2/ C. A few metres to the right is an open sloping face. Scramble straight up for 50m, easier on the right. Reach a bushy slope and follow this up and left.

3/ C+. Follow the obvious route through a gully to a small nek dominated by a mature Hottentot cherry tree. Ascend directly up the ridge via an awkward 'C' move in a small corner at 20m.

4/ The route now ends by a scramble, easier on the right, up a sloping slab of rock leading to the top.

Bridge Wings.
10. Nigel Peddie, Mary Peddie. Date 1990

The take-off is strenuous and is from a prominent convenient rock

1/ 13m 10. Follow the steep diagonal to the left to reach a very secure stance between conspicuous rock wings, which inspired the route name.

2/ 20m 10. Follow a long arc clockwise into the corner beneath an overhanging roof. From here move upwards and right, round the nose and then climb 4m straight up to a comfortable belay stance.

3/ 16m 10. Continue straight up through a conspicuous gap and then climb onto the rock on the left. Step over the gap, then climb up and around the corner to finish straight up to the top.

4/ A short scramble takes one onto the 'Hawse Pipe route. Where the climber can descend to the right.

The Hottentots Anomaly

On the 17th May 2016 I was taking part in a hike whilst walking on some of the high jeep tracks below the Hottentots Holland Rim when I looked up and saw a circular arrangement of boulders high up on the hillside that had no logical business being there.

The May 2016 sighting of the boulder circle

On my return home to Sir Lowry's Pass I scanned Google Earth for any sign of the anomaly, and there, just below the high track, bisected by an almost perfect south to north trajectory, was a semicircle of boulders with what looked like a debris field beyond it.

Curiosity piqued, I began an intensive period of research, which saw me reading papers and listening to many online lectures on land slips, sink holes, river ox bows, talus slopes and their depositions.

Site Visits
We were fortunate in gaining the support of the estate concerned, and together with the estate ecological officer, two experienced geologists Brent Jellocoe and Kobus Theron, along with expertise from a local University, we began a series of site visits.

Over late 2016 we visited the site several times, mapping and taking measurements of the depression.

Understanding Scree and Talus
'Scree Is a collection of broken rock fragments at the base of crags, mountain cliffs, volcanoes or valley shoulders that has accumulated through periodic rock fall from adjacent cliff faces.

Landforms associated with these materials are often called talus deposits. Talus deposits typically have a concave upwards form, while the maximum inclination corresponds to the angle of repose of the mean debris size.

One is dramatically tempted to immediately assume that it is a meteorite impact crater or near ground meteor explosion, though there are other more plausible explanations.

Talus at the bottom of Mount Yamnuska, Alberta, Canada

Possible Causes:
Meteorite strike
Over the millennia there have of course been many million meteorite strikes on planet Earth. They are thought to have brought certain amino acids and cells to earth that could have been the seeds of life. They also brought water so essential to life. They also brought several cataclysmic extinction events, one of which is thought to have caused the end of 70 million years of the dinosaur's rule.

Over billions of years, the planet surface has changed continually. This ongoing upheaval and movement caused by the action of tectonic plates has erased all but the most recent – in geological terms – impact sites. Estimates vary but the consensus seems to be that there are only some 180 visible meteorite impact sights on the planet earth. Any additions to the list are of interest to the scientific community, but must be verified by hard evidence including:

1) There should be the sign or remnants of a crater.
2) There should be a debris cone outside the crater.
3) Rock samples should be taken, examination of which must show signs of heat deformation and shatter cone structures, caused by the original impact explosion.

Potholes and Sink holes
A pothole, in geologic terms, is a hole that is worn into the bedrock of a stream in strong rapids or at the base of a waterfall. As the flowing water swirls into eddies, the force of the water spins rock fragments, sand and gravel, scoured out a small indentation in the bedrock. This debris gets caught in the eddies and essentially acts as a drill, boring down into the rock. After years and years of constant drilling, the stones and sands carve a cylindrical hole.

Pothole Formation

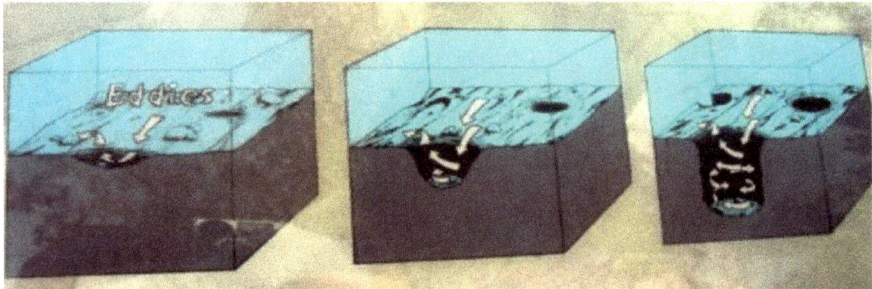

Sink Hole Formation
Sinkholes form in sedimentary rocks that are susceptible to ground water solutioning such as limestone and salt, which creates somewhat circular depressions and collapse features.

Given that the immediate surface area of the feature is at moderately high elevation on an actively eroding slope, and that it is located either on marine shales and sandstone beds of the lowermost Peninsula Formation, or on scree covering the underlying bedrock of Cape Granite Suite, there is no real evidence for either of these geological origins.

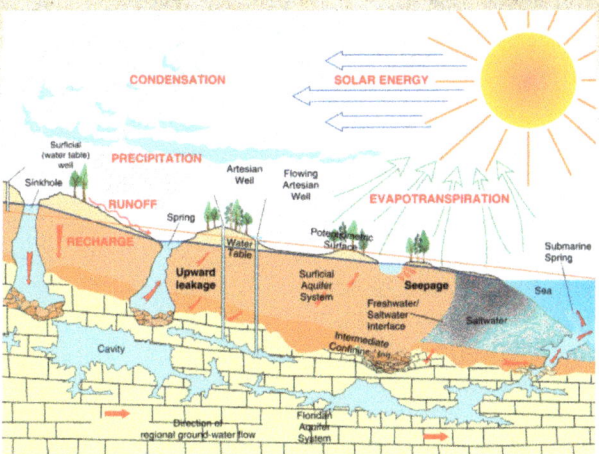

Water wash, old 'Oxbow'

The nearest streams of any size are those that flow from the Sneeukop Gorge more than a kilometre to the north-west, and from the Landdroskop gorge half a kilometer to the south east. If this were a water wash event, the river flow would have to have been considerable, and be one that emanated from a source that is no longer visible.

Bearing in mind that the anomaly is geologically young, we should have been able to see evidence of any such water flow source.

Land Slips / Natural geological process

Of the possible 'other causes' this would appear to be the most plausible. There is natural shelving in the local rock that might lend itself to the slope in front of the 'crater' and the cone/shelf above.

There is also a natural spring in the centre of the depression, that would add lubrication to the possibly already water saturated talus slope above.

Landslips are caused by the movement downslope of a mass of rock, debris, earth, or soil (soil being a mixture of earth and debris). Landslides occur when gravitational and other types of shear stresses within a slope exceed the shear strength (resistance to shearing) of the materials that form the slope.

Shear stresses can be built up within a slope by several processes. These include over steepening of the base of the slope, such as by natural erosion or excavation, and loading of the slope, such as by an inflow of water and/or a rise in the groundwater table.

Age of anomaly

There are two main parameters to work on.

1/ The fact that the anomaly exists at all on a slope undergoing continual erosion – as already noted, would indicate that the site postdates the creation of the surrounding topography. Its delineation remains clear, having suffered little from any erosion, which in geological terms indicates it happened 'yesterday'. Though in terms of years this would indicate any time up to 100,000 years ago.

2/ The second indicator that tells us the incident could not have been caused any more recently than roughly 3,000 years ago is the nature of the 'crater' centre.

As already noted, initially there is likely to have been a small pool, due to the 'crater' hollow being lower than the water table. This lake slowly filled with vegetation until it disappeared, leaving us now with a mass of waterlogged material. This accumulation must have taken a considerable time.

Based purely on 'feel' the event is between 3,000 to 15,000 years old.

Any of my notes above are subject to expert correction.

In conclusion

Though the case for a landslip - caused by a saturated slope, exacerbated by a ground spring at its base providing additional lubrication - seems overwhelming. Some geologists have lingering doubts due to the elliptical symmetry of the anomaly's shape, and by the complete lack of any debris 'wave' in the 'run out' area below.

Whatever the cause of the Hottentots Holland Anomaly, the ensuing rumble that must have taken place, would have given cause to wonder for any nearby early tribes' people.

References:

www.geocaching.com/geocache/GC4GAVP_caps-ridge-potholes?guid=f70ce19f-530a-475b-895b-5c6ee19994a3
https://en.wikipedia.org/wiki/File:Florida_groundwater_cycle.gif

Picture courtesy of Kobus Theron

Basic Guide to Evac / Rescue Procedure

In the event of an emergency whilst on a hike, the following is a general guide.

Bear in mind that actions stated here may or may not be possible on a case by case basis.

Start of Hike
1/ At the start of a hike, ask who is medically qualified. It could be a 1st Aid Cert, nurse, or medical doctor. If none present, the Leader and Sweep will assume responsibility.

At time of Incident
1/ Try to obtain any medical history.
2/ Any known medications being taken.
3/ Any indications by the patient that they were in difficulty before the incident / collapse.
4/ Only if trained, and if necessary, administer CPR.
5/ Ascertain level of consciousness - A) Any reaction to sound - answers questions, B) Reacts to pain / pinch the patient, C) Totally unconsciousness.
6/ Apply 1st Aid as appropriate.
7/ Gather 2 -3 people around you who are willing and able to assist.
8/ Move the rest of the party well away. Appoint a leader of this second group. They must still be looked after.

Communications to Rescue Services (RS)
1/ Call 021 937 0300, have this number on your phone prefixed by AAA. Always speak calmly and clearly.
2/ Give the RS any relevant details from 1 to 6 above.
3/ Have at least two Grid Reference (GR) Apps on your phone, and cross check with others that the GR is correct. You may be asked to send a 'pin'.
4/ Pass the GR and description of your location.
5/ Be aware that you may have to move to a higher point - line of sight - in order to get a call out.
6/ Be aware that your GR App works off satellites and not from a cell signal. You may get a GR when you can't get a call out to the RS's.
7/ If using sight or sound to raise an alarm, six torch flashes and/or six whistle blasts is the international distress call.
8/ The signal that this has been received is three flashes or whistle blasts.

On the approach of a helicopter
1/ Have one person stand with their back to the wind with arms stretched up in a 'V' position facing the best landing site / casualty evacuation point. This will assist the pilot to see ground direction and where to land / lower the stretcher. Be aware that the pilot may choose another evacuation point.
2/ If possible, have a space blanket available to position in the centre of the best landing / stretcher lower point. Weigh this down very well. This will also assist the pilot to find you.
3/ Make sure there is nothing that can be blown away, hats, rucksacs etc. The helicopter down draft is very strong. Also, items can be sucked into the air intake.
4/ The helicopter may lower an earthing strop. This must not be touched until it has reached the ground. The winch man will direct you by signs as to what he/she wants you to do.
5/ The stretcher will be lowered / taken out from the helicopter with an attendant / rescue team. The rescue team will be in charge. All their requests must be followed.

Written by Steve Chadwick in consultation with WSAR,

Snake bite first aid

This article is a precis by Steve Chadwick taken with permission from a longer text by Johan Marais to concentrate on our Western cape snakes

" *First-aid: most of the familiar methods for first-aid treatment of snakebite, both western and "traditional/herbal", have been found to result in more harm than good and should be firmly discouraged*"

With the rise of social media, the endless old wives' tales, myths, and general bad advice on the topic has progressed these into believable advice, The most important thing to do in the event of a snakebite is to get the patient to the closest medical facility urgently and safely. The first choice is always the closest hospital that has a trauma unit, but this is not always possible.

At the African Snakebite Institute, we are inundated with calls and emails asking what hospitals carry antivenom. Nobody knows, as a hospital may obtain antivenom today, use it tonight and never replace it. But that is not the big issue. When someone is bitten by a highly venomous snake, the biggest danger is that the person may die from a lack of oxygen. In Black Mamba or Cape Cobra bites, the victim may have trouble with breathing well within an hour. Mouth-to-mouth resuscitation could well be lifesaving. (Steve note - usually vetinary clinics carry antivenom as curious dogs regularly get bitten).

Well over 90% of all serious snakebites in our area are from snakes with potent cytotoxic venom – Puff Adder, Rhombic Night Adder and the Stiletto Snake being the main culprits. In such bites there is very little that the first aider can do, as cytotoxic venom causes severe pain and swelling that spreads slowly and may result in blistering and tissue damage. Such a patient needs to be taken to a medical facility, as the early administration of antivenom, if required, will reduce the extent of tissue damage. Bear in mind that only one out of ten snakebite patients that are hospitalised require and receive antivenom.

Boomslang bites are rare and their venom affects the blood clotting mechanism. In a known boomslang bite, do not apply any bandages and get the patient to a medical facility.

If you are dealing with a snakebite with immediate pain and swelling, loosen tight clothing, remove rings and bracelets and avoid all bandages. While transporting the patient you can slightly elevate the affected limb – just above the heart. It has little effect on the outcome of such a bite but will bring pain relief.

The life-threatening bites are from snakes with predominantly neurotoxic venom, and in the Cape the main culprit is the Cape Cobra. Other cobras like the Snouted Cobra and Forest Cobra have neurotoxins in their venom, but usually have their fair share of cytotoxins as well and the onset of symptoms is not that dramatic.

Very soon after a bite from a Cape Cobra, patients often mention numbness of the lips, a metallic taste in the mouth, difficulty with swallowing, nausea and excessive sweating. As they become progressively weaker, ptosis (droopy eye lids), dilated pupils and difficulty swallowing may be seen. The breathing becomes heavier and heavier until the patient stops breathing.

Pressure Pad
In a confirmed Cape Cobra bite on a limb one can immediately put a pressure pad on the bite or just above it towards the heart. Such a pad could consist of a piece of cotton wool and should be bandaged as tightly as one would a sprained ankle. Such a pressure pad may trap the venom in that area and delay the rate at which it spreads and does damage. Experiments on pressure pads have been done for more than 40 years and with good results.

Pressure Immobilisation
The initial idea of pressure bandages for neurotoxic envenomation came about in the late 70s when Dr. Sutherland from Australia experimented with pressure bandages. His hypothesis was that initially, most of the venom is absorbed through the lymphatic system, and by putting pressure on lymphatics, he demonstrated that venom absorption and subsequent symptoms were delayed. Pressure immobilisation is now used throughout the world.

The biggest problem with pressure immobilisation is that a specific pressure is required for such bandages to have any effect – around 50 – 70 mmHg – and achieving that pressure is no easy task. Having said that, we now have bandages with rectangles printed on them, and when the bandage is stretched so that the rectangles become squares, and applied so, the correct amount of pressure is achieved. The pressure then averages around 60 mmHg. One always starts wrapping the bandage on the site of the bite and then the limb is wrapped towards the heart. Once applied, the patient must be kept as still as possible as muscle movement stimulates the lymphatics. (Steve note - a crepe bandage correctly applied will do).

Arterial Tourniquets
Arterial tourniquets can be extremely dangerous and are not recommended for snakebite. Sadly, most rural people immediately apply a tourniquet after a snakebite using a belt, shoelace, clothing or even fence wire, and in many cases such tourniquets do a great deal of damage. Patients have lost limbs and others have died because of tourniquets.

There is definite evidence that incorrectly applied and managed tourniquets are dangerous, especially in cases of local necrosis where a tourniquet may result in the confining of venom locally.

Assist-breathing

Snakebite victims that die soon after a bite, do so as a result of a lack of breathing. It is of utmost importance to assist the breathing of a patient by use of CPR and by using a pocket mask.

———————————————

Steve is a City of Cape Town registered snake catch and release person.

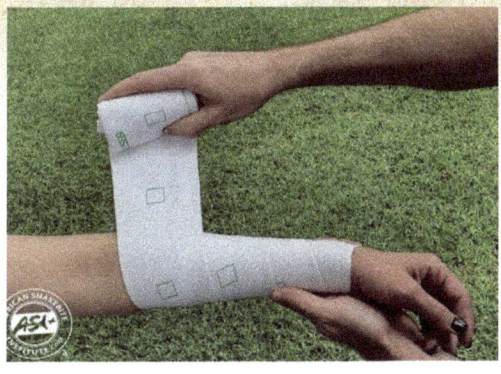

Pressure bandages should not be applied in cases of cytotoxic or haemotoxic envenomation. Once applied, leave the bandage in place until the patient reaches a medical centre.

simple one-way pocket mask to assist breathe a patient.

This simple and inexpensive device seals well over the mouth and nose of an adult and if inverted can also be used on an infant. It has a one-way valve to protect the rescue breather from ingesting bodily fluids and in adults you will give one breath every six seconds.

Heat Exhaustion

A - Day before your hike.
Two factors have the most effect in increasing the risk of HE.

1/ Humidity. Most forecast Apps give the expected humidity. A typical reading might be - 80% humidity and a temperature of 18 deg around early morning.

Humidity will fall slowly during the day to reach a typical mid-afternoon point of 50%.
The higher the humidity, the less your body is able to sweat effectively; and you need to sweat!

Counter intuitive - as you will lose body water when you sweat - but the fact is that losing moisture by sweat is a major factor in the body's ability to maintain an even temperature, as moisture evaporates from your skin.

2/ Outside temperature. Again, your Apps will tell you the forecast temperature. As we know different forecasts can vary alarmingly, so to be safe, take the higher reading.

So, the day before you go on your hike add the two together to get the Heat Index. The nearer you get to 90, the more danger there is of HE.

Do the maths - 07:00hrs 83% humidity + 17deg = Heat Index of 100. This is why, although cooler in the morning, you will still sweat so much, and you can overheat on that early ascent.

Maths at 14:00hrs 65% humidity + 31deg = 96. Less humidity but higher temperature, plus - if you are standing in full sunshine the Heat Index will be even higher.

If both Heat Index figures are above 90 - unless you take precautions, there is a real danger one or more of your party will suffer from HE. .

B - Morning of your hike.
1/ The alarm goes off. Feed the cat and have breakfast. Every bit of moisture you put into your body will assist you especially when you are on the first part of your hike, which often entails a hot sweaty climb. Try not to have coffee - this is a diuretic and will increase the body's tendency to expel water through urination. Try to have a glass of water when you wake. More water as you eat breakfast. And even though you don't feel like it - drink another glass of water just before you leave the house. This will give your body a supply of water when you really need it for that sweaty early climb.

2/ Preparation for the water you carry. In the summer I carry two litres. Often the hike description will tell you if you can expect water en-route. Nevertheless carry at least two litres.

As your body sweats it depletes your body's salt supply leading sometimes to debilitating muscle cramps. I add a pinch of salt to each litre. Not enough to spoil the taste, but I have found it really helps in fighting cramps, not just during the hike, but also in the evening when cramps often strike.

C - During the hike.

Water is better inside your body than inside your rucksack. Yes, you have to spread it across the hike, but top up at breather stops as you make that initial climb.

I wear a vest that will wick sweat away from my body. Cotton and other natural fibres do not do this well. Look in outdoor shops with vests or shirts that advertise wicking ability.

Cotton T shirts are hydrophilic and absorb your sweat and do not want to let it go. Cotton sweatshirts slow your body's ability to cool.

Obviously, a wide brimmed hat. It not only takes the sweat from my head and stops sweat going in my eyes. The wide brim also keeps the sun from your head and neck and also increases wicking and evaporation. A baseball type hat does not protect you except to keep the sun from your eyes.

Indications of HE:

Confusion,	Fatigue	Plan skin
Dark yellow urine.	Headache	Profuse sweating
Dizziness	Muscle cramps	Rapid Heartbeat.
Fainting	Nausea	

First signs that as hikers, we usually see on the hill.

Dark urine - Typically as your kidneys filter out waste products from stressed muscles your urine will become dark yellow, indicating an imbalance, and your body is saying I need more water to get back to a nice straw coloured yellow.

Cramps - usually in the major leg muscles. Indicating the body's lack of salts, electrolytes and other trace minerals.

Dizziness - which can lead to a stumbling / falling accident.

The hike leader must look out for these symptoms, also the whole hike group must (and invariably does) look out for other members of the group.

Treatment:
- Drink plenty of fluids. Sports drinks can be useful to replace lost minerals (avoid alcohol and energy drinks with caffeine). Carry rehydration powders in your 1st aid kit.

- Move patient into shade or provide shade by placing spare clothing across bushes and/or hiking poles.

- Offer the patient Crampeze - or other similar product. The patient has the right to refuse any medication you offer. Cramp tabs have an almost miraculously quick effect in easing cramped muscles.

- Remove any tight or unnecessary clothing.

- Apply other cooling measures such as fanning and cold wet towels.
- Reassure the patient.

Some of us carry a small container holding a little water and a special towel. We take out the towel and shake it vigorously. This causes the towel to cool and can be put on the patient.

Best cooling points are the major blood supplies where any cooling will have the best effect on lowering body temperature.

Front and back of the neck. Forehead. Hands. Do what you can to cool these areas.

Face the patient forward and pour a little water over the head. This will aid heat loss through evaporation.

After recovery, take the patient down the easiest way from your hike.

I have not touched on Heat Stroke, which is much more serious, as when hiking we will usually see HE first.

Obviously make use of stops during the hike in shady places, and or in any breeze that you may find.

Looking into the future, dehydrating your body can have longer term debilitating effects. Lack of sufficient water passing through the kidneys allowing that organ to do its cleansing work, may lead to a build-up of salt and minerals that can coalesce into stones. When these stones pass through the urinary tract it gives a pain such that you will really wish you had drunk more water.

www.ingramcontent.com/pod-product-compliance
Lightning Source LLC
Chambersburg PA
CBHW050816090426
42736CB00021B/3471